Woozel, Boxing and Me
A look at the funny side of boxing

by
Rusty Rubin

Bloomington, IN  Milton Keynes, UK

AuthorHouse™
1663 Liberty Drive, Suite 200
Bloomington, IN 47403
www.authorhouse.com
Phone: 1-800-839-8640

AuthorHouse™ UK Ltd.
500 Avebury Boulevard
Central Milton Keynes, MK9 2BE
www.authorhouse.co.uk
Phone: 08001974150

© *2006 Rusty Rubin. All rights reserved.*

No part of this book may be reproduced, stored in a retrieval system, or transmitted by any means without the written permission of the author.

First published by AuthorHouse 7/24/2006

ISBN: 1-4259-2574-X (sc)

Printed in the United States of America
Bloomington, Indiana

This book is printed on acid-free paper.

In loving memory of my soul mate Mary Susan Walker (Susiey, Woozel), 9/17/49 – 2/19/04. Let this book serve to honor her memory throughout eternity.

Contents

Introduction		ix
Round I	The Insanity Begins	1
Round II	Boxing bits and pieces.	31
Round III	Ring Humor and More	49
Round IV	More About Woozel	65
Round V	It's not all that great	83
Round VI	Funny and True	99
Round VII	Woozel Bwain	119
Round VIII	The High and the Flighty	133
Round IX	The Punchline	149
Round X	More from Callahan and Peter Palmiere	165
Big-Ups		173
Round XI	One Crazy Business	187
Round XII	The Final Bell	201

INTRODUCTION

I DECIDED TO write this book to share many memories, including funny stories, true short stories (oddities) and funny quotes, to help improve the image of boxing, one of the oldest of all known sports. Also boxing is the one sport that probably needs the improvement the most.

To the best of my knowledge, all the stories contained herein are true. You would need the world's greatest imagination to make up many of them.

I've been blessed, not with money or great looks, but the ability to make lasting friendships and I have experienced the powerful emotions of true love among my relationships. Happiness to me is not working 9-5 jobs, I leave that for other people, and it's not having kids and sending them off to college or war or to make babies. I had three children and like myself, I've tried to give them a strong sense of values and what they do with that gift will be their own choice.

Happiness to me is living my life on my terms, and with the people I want to be with. I've learned that the saying 'to thy own self be true', is meant for people like myself.

I had always wanted to be a sports writer and broadcast journalist, as well as write books. With the love and support of my loving wife Lois, and my many friends, I have been able to achieve these dreams.

And I've been able to have all these learning experiences and more, without ever having to intentionally hurt anyone, as I always endeavor to be up front and honest with everyone I deal with. How many people can say that they truly believe they found the meaning of life? The Lord has truly blessed me.

Glove2Glove, which is a non-denominational prayer group, which I set up, to have people who are interested, said prayers for Sue and other boxing people in need. Some members, who never even spoke to her, sent her cards and flowers. Many of these fine people have also joined my circle of friends. We never asked for money because prayer is free and at least in my eyes, and others, even more important than money to our high calling.

While the implicit purpose of this book is to bring some laughter to those who need it (just about everyone), I had to use some chapters to explain my long-time best bud, Sue, who was by my side during many of these humorous experiences, and in truth created many of them herself. As a person who truly believes that laughter extends longevity as well as the quality of life, I credit Sue for my longevity (as well as my wife, Lois, and her medical insurance) for allowing me some extra years on this earth. Although without Sue, who passed away in 2004, life just hasn't been as much fun as it once was.

Still, the extra years have allowed me to finish this book, a final tribute to a very special young lady.

So I ask the readers indulgence when reading the opening chapter, just so they can fully understand and appreciate the happenings in the chapters of this book that I have devoted to, for want of a better word, goofiness.

To appreciate all these stories you have to understand (or try to) Wuzzel. And believe me; it would be hard enough even if you didn't read the opening chapter. What more you say about Sue, a life-loving gal who felt that the most romantic place I ever brought her to was ALCATRAZ? She was so taken by the Island/prison that she even wanted to return the next day with sandwiches and camp out overnight.

Sue also would bite her nails, but not just her finger nails. She actually used to bite her toe-nails. I guess that got harder as she aged, and instead she decided to bring a large knife in her carry on, to the airport, *after the September 11th tragedy* (story included in this book).

Allow me to dedicate this book, in its entirety, to both Wuz and my wonderful wife Lois, who put up with me/us all of the time, although like most people, she never quite understood Sue either. In truth, it wasn't hard, Sue just wanted to live life on her terms and play life's game by her rules, and she never hurt anyone, except ultimately herself.

I owe Lois a lot more than this, for if it weren't for her, there may not have been the unforgettable memories, a Ringsports.com magazine, a website by the same name, and the books I have written.

As I stated, I was blessed with the best wife, as well as the best friends that anyone could ever want. I was twice blessed because I was able to fulfill my life's dreams of being, a sportswriter, a sportscaster, and an author, and now, all three of my dreams at the same time. Most important to me, was to be able work for myself, as I've always been too damn independent to take orders from anyone.

Special thanks to Pauline Reese, a good friend, who took the time to proofread and edit this manuscript, she among many others in my life serve to prove how wonderful people can be.

And I have been blessed in many ways, not to mention (which I will in the pages ahead) the best gifts that all the money in the world cannot buy, love and laughter.

If the Lord saw fit to take me tomorrow, I may have few, if any regrets, and I would change little, except for the people I may have inadvertently hurt along the way. With the help of my wife and friends I was able to live my life's dream, and how many people can say that?

Add to that the many awards I have garnered, which while I sincerely appreciate, comes in second to all the wonderful friends I've made in and out of the world of boxing. Second only to God's love, these are and always will be, my greatest treasures.

It was a combination of the Lord's help, and all of these great friends, as I started, what I feel is my greatest accomplishment in boxing,

"Glove2Glove", a non-profit (like everything else that I've done in this lifetime) was my way of returning back to society a bit of what I have been given. I was never involved in boxing for its monetary benefits (never realized any) or for the awards that probably should have gone to others more deserving than myself.

I was never involved in boxing just for the sport. I was involved because the people in boxing, including most of the die-hard fans, are hard-working blue collar folks, who, when they become your friend, would give you the shirt off their backs in the middle of a New England winter. They are in my humble opinion, some of the greatest people on Earth.

To be sure, there are a few that take advantage of others, using boxing as a way to create great wealth, even if it sometimes comes through illegal means. Those people, some sadly in the boxing hierarchy, in my experience, make up little more than one percent of the people in boxing. If that percentage is much higher, I'll be in for a huge shock.

I've often said that boxing is a microcosm of our society. We have all the drama, action, corruption at times, and certainly a lot of politics. The boxing world is, in every sense, a copy of the outside one.

I wanted to have a few other stories used in this book, but I couldn't reach the always funny Tex Cobb, who I was told picks up his messages at a bar in Philadelphia, and others who I was able to reach but couldn't find the time to sit down with them. Bert Sugar, an old and dear friend was also too involved in a project to help out, which I knew he would have done otherwise.

Thanks to all my friends who made contributions to this book. And special thanks to Derek Callahan for his tireless help in acquiring a lot of interesting stories for this manuscript.

Most of all, thank you Lois, for designing this cover and for being the best wife ever; and thank you Sue for being yourself, thereby making this book possible, and thanks to all my other friends for making this true labor of love a reality. Most importantly, I thank the Lord for giving me the talent and the many opportunities to be able to live my life on my terms.

As I said, I've truly been blessed.

Round I

The Insanity Begins

I FIRST MET Susiey "Woozel" Walker, (her real first name was Mary, but, like many of us, she much preferred being called by another name, (in this case her given first name) early in 1981.

Eileen, my wife at the time, introduced me to her friend Sue and her only son, Dorian, who was 13 at the time. We ate lunch and shared some laughs at a local casino, the Gold Dust West, in Reno, NV. I can't say I had any strong feelings one way or another for Wuz at that time, except that she was very pretty, peppy and funny and she had a beautiful Southern twang to her soft voice. For although she was born in Washington D.C., her family was originally from West Virginia.

THERE WAS ABSOLUTELY NO doubt in my mind that Wuz had the looks to be a supermodel or a movie star. In my eyes at least, she was drop dead gorgeous. But alas Wuz wasn't one of those gals who took photographed well. Almost all of the ones she took never did her justice. Believe me, I take damn good pictures and few of any of the ones I shot of her turned

The Insanity Begins

out the way they should have. It was the same problem with some true professionals who took her picture; Sue just would never photograph well.

I immediately knew that Sue was also a bit different then most folks because she would spell her name Susiey. I had never heard of anyone spelling it that way before, and I thought I had heard all the spellings of the name. But that was Wuz; if anything was considered conventional it was absolutely not her style.

BEFORE I GET much further along, I'd better explain to the readers exactly what a Woozel is, at least to my way of thinking.

When I had first met Sue, Eileen, was working with and was very friendly to her as well. Eileen had told me that Sue had a somewhat questionable reputation and she would often joke when speaking about her, "Susiey Woozie, she's a floozy". Well, Woozie was to become Woozel, and that then evolved into Wuzzel and Wuz, the nicknames that I gave to her, and it stuck. Sue, not understanding the rational for her new pet name, asked me early on about her new nickname. "Is that Woozel as in weasel?" I laughed, "No, Sue. It's Woozel, as in love".

ON JUNE 5, 1985, I awoke in a pool of sweat and realized the powerful emotions that I suddenly felt towards Sue. I told my close friends of my never before felt emotions, and they all said the same things, that my feelings towards Wuz was nothing more then infatuation or puppy love, and it soon would pass. Boy where they ever off base. The dynamics of my feelings did change for Sue over the years, but the intensity of them has never passed and obviously never will.

Woozel, Boxing and Me

AT THE TIME we met, Sue was 30, 5'3" about 130 lbs., and a very, very attractive brunette with hazel eyes, a great sense of humor and an infectious laugh and a body that would turn on any normal person, which of course, initially had left me out. Besides, being very unhappily married at the time, with three young children, I certainly wasn't going to fool around, especially with someone who worked with and was friends with my wife.

SUE AND I met for a second time in June of that year, when my wife's father passed away, and Eileen returned to her home in Brooklyn, NY, for the funeral. Sue called when Eileen was gone to tell me that she had baked some chocolate chip cookies for me and my three kids (who I was watching until Eileen would return from her sad mission east).

I picked the cookies up from Sue at her work, JC Penney's. Once again, there was nothing special; I thanked her for the bag of delicious treats and took them home to the kids. But then I remembered that two of them were hyperactive and I kind of felt a bit guilty about giving them so much chocolate, so I did the noble thing and ate most of them myself. I was always happy to step up and bravely protect my children.

AS THE SAYING GOES, 'three's a charm', and it was the third time I met Sue, as I have related previously, June 5, 1985, a day that will live forever in my memory, and has become very, very special to me, although physically absolutely nothing was to happen between us. Sue called and told me that she wanted to make a chicken casserole and salad for me and the kids to enjoy and I told her that would be fine. I didn't want to disappoint my wife's friend and at 200 plus pounds, how could I refuse?

Sue decided to bring all the ingredients up to the house and cook the food there. Eileen was still in Brooklyn, so Sue's generosity saved me the chore of cooking. Sue drove up to our house, prepared a delicious full course meal and left to be with her boyfriend at the time, Jim, who I later came to find out was an alcoholic, and who was also her boss at work. This would serve to explain how this was had been the one job that she not only was able to keep, or at least wanted to.

It was early the next morning, about 3 AM, on June 6, that I awoke, drenched in perspiration, my heart beating rapidly, and realized that I was head over heals in love with that woman. It was as if I was suddenly struck by a lightning bolt. And it was a feeling that I knew at once would stay with me for the rest of my life. It has. And I'm sure that it will continue even longer.

WUZ HAD BECOME my Angel. Not an Angel always, behavior wise, but my Angel none the less. She had her faults, as we all do. But the laughter that we would share for more than twenty-five years, far exceeded and made up for any shortcomings, the biggest of which was her mood swings. Her emotional sings, highs and lows which could drive me, and probably even a trained psychiatrist, crazy.

BUT THE REALITY at that time was that Wuz had a crush on Jim, (I'm not convinced it wasn't more of a martyr complex) her boss at J.C. Penney's Outlet Store. Like her husband at the time, Don, (they were separated), Jim was both a womanizer and an alcoholic.

Don has long-since re-married and moved to Las Vegas, and to his great credit, has turned his life completely around. He no longer drinks or fools around, and goes to church regularly with his new wife. I know that it could not have been easy for him to do this, but quite understandable when you know that all that boozing and womanizing probably cost him his marriage to Sue, which up till that point at least, was probably the best thing that had ever happened to him.

His new wife was able to get him involved in going to church on a regular basis, which certainly didn't hurt either.

He was always a hard worker, even when he was drinking. He knew his responsibilities and lived up to them.

And while it's very hard to pinpoint exactly when Sue started her drinking, (Wuz did have a bit of a problem with it as well, particularly when depressed). She did tell me that she began to drink just after her father had passed away, and she felt badly that she had to return to Yerington, NV. (About an hour and a half drive from, where she was living with Don), to take care of her son.

As a result she wasn't at her father's bedside at the time of his death. Her father Thomas was both a drinker and a smoker, and Sue's 'pal', and he passed away from lung cancer. I was told by her mom and sister that Sue was just like her father.

EILEEN, MY WIFE AT THE TIME, Eileen, and I went to an apartment that Sue and Jim had rented for a short time. We played the 'Newlywed Game', and Jim, (who later, according to Sue) returned late from a bout of womanizing) came home late. and the food she had prepared had gotten cold.

To get even Sue changed from her jeans into tight black panties that she wore under a short skirt, so she could show off her many beautiful feminine charms to me, when she eagerly and intentionally did every time she bent over. She would do this often on this evening to upset Jim.

Jim was also pissed when playing the game because Sue and I had far more knowledge (we were partners) of each other then they (Eileen and Jim) did, and Jim was my ex-wife's boss as well.

THE VAST KNOWLEDGE Wuz and I had of each other was something that had to be carried over from a previous lifetime together, or maybe a lot more then one. In the eyes of most of the people who knew us, Sue and I were the perfect couple. Most people, except for Sue.

The Insanity Begins

WUZ COULD ALSO get a bit abusive towards me, when drinking heavily. Because she knew how I felt about her, Sue would keep testing me, knowing that I would never abuse her. So, I unintentionally became her whipping boy. I didn't like it, but I didn't want to risk losing her either. Fortunately for me that stage was going to leave town very quickly.

IN FACT WUZ and I seemed to have almost everything in common, short of my writing talent and our tastes in music and TV, (different generation, I was seven plus years older). Our tastes in movies differed a bit, as I preferred comedy and she liked the macabre.

But we both loved eating spicy food, animals, eating out often, hanging out, traveling, and just having fun together. In truth just being together was almost always fun because we were able to play off each other very well.

SUE WASN'T THE only one who had a goofy life before we met. When Eileen was pregnant, and we were living in New York, she went into labor and a friend Claudia, and I jumped in my car to take her to the hospital. Of course we had driven about three blocks before we realized that Eileen wasn't with us. We turned around and picked her up, leaning against a garbage can.

FOR A BRIEF time, when I was living in New York, I took a job as a driving instructor. One of the oddest stories here was when I had an elderly Jewish woman for a student. This nice lady with a heavy accent seemed to prefer companionship rather than actually learning how to drive.

We were heading up a one way street, when we came to a stop sign and on the opposite corner a sign that said "All Traffic" with an arrow pointing to the left. The lady stopped at the stop sign for more than a minute, than looked at me and said" "Mr. Rubin, I vant to esk you a qvestion". I asked her what, to which she promptly replied: "Am I treffic?" Thinking she was joking, I said, 'of course not, you're a car'. At which time she stepped on the gas and proceeded to go straight ahead on a one way street heading in the wrong direction. There was a police car parked on the one way street, but fortunately no one was in it.***

AND ANOTHER TIME IN NYC when I was co-managing a political campaign, we were doing a fund raiser for the candidate. I asked a local supporter who happened to be an alcoholic to get some flowers to use as place settings for the tables. I told him to bill it to the campaign. During the introduction speech I was making, my campaign co-manager called me over: "The table settings" he whispered. "What about them", I inquired. "Poison ivy" he responded. The volunteer had decided to pick the place settings instead of spending campaign money on them.

    I looked into the crowd and noticed that many of them were scratching, I excused myself, walked off the podium till I could regain my composure, which lasted until someone in the audience asked if they can keep the place settings. I was barely able to say that 'anyone who wants them can keep them', before thinking about it and apologized by saying that 'the place settings must be returned'.***

SUE ALWAYS HAD DOGS as did her mom and older sister Marion. When I first met her, she had a beautiful Irish Setter named Jinx (after her older brothers nickname) and Jinx was as smart as a whip, but like all of us, she reached a time where her suffering was so great it showed that life had to end, and the dog had to be put down.

    Although it was the humane thing to do, this was very hard on Sue, and since she was with her abusive boyfriend, Joe, at that time, I wasn't afforded much time to give her very much solace. The evening that she put Jinx down, Sue went alone to the Sands Casino, got totally shit-faced, and had to be put in jail for the night, just for protective custody.

SUE AND I had to have been together in a previous life, probably more than one, because from the start we had a relationship based on genuine trust, understanding and companionship, (but sadly rarely love, at least on her part), from the get-go. To cite just one example, when Wuz got an inheritance check of almost $18,000, and had some extra funds, she turned the check over to me to invest for her, put it in my name, and I did help make her a lot of money.

Although Sue knew that I was down on my luck at that point of time, and out of work, Wuz just walked into my studio apartment, plopped the check on my table and signed it over to me.

As I said, there was never a question of trust between us.

Sue knew that I was pretty well versed on the stock market, having worked on Wall Street for more then a year. I did insist however, that before I touch any of the money, she must take the time and learn what to look for before we invested one dime, as I had never expected to outlive her. It took a couple of long nights, but Sue now knew just about as much about the stock market (or almost) as I did. I made sure of that, particularly as to what drove the market at that time, supply and demand, not anticipated earnings as it has become today.

WUZ HAD ANOTHER DOG, which her sister Marion had to put down soon after Sue passed away. That dogs name was also Jinx and she was a very smart Pit Bull. Problem was it had serious health problems, was 9 years old, didn't get along with other dogs and being a pit bull, no one wanted to adopt it.

I really liked that dog a lot and Jinx and I were pals, but she didn't get along with our (my wife Lois and my remaining dog, Moo,) or her sisters two dogs, and unfortunately that had to become the bottom line. Jinx had to be put down. I know that all her beloved animals are in Heaven with Sue now, as I eventually hope to be also.

One of the annuals must-do's for Sue and I happened every Christmas season, when we took her pit bull Jinx to Reno's Park Lane Mall to get a picture of the dog, sitting on Santa's lap. Dogs weren't allowed in the mall, but of course nothing was going to stop Wuz, security guards or not.. I don't think that Santa Claus was eagerly looking forward to having a pit bull sitting on his lap, even if only long enough to take a picture.

LOOKING BACK, IT'S easy now (but didn't make any sense then) for me to understand why Sue had once told me when I asked her to marry me. "I could never marry you, you're not my type of man". As it turned out, she was right, and while I could easily hold my own drinking with most, (as long as the drinks weren't mixed) I certainly wasn't an alcoholic, I didn't do drugs, and I certainly would never hit a woman. Still, if I had a buck for every time that I asked her to be my wife, I'd be a rich man today.

Her type of man turned out to be a Joe, a druggie, who beat her up, caused a detached retina and left her for dead in a pool of blood. Or a Jim, who was a jealous alcoholic and who always checked up on her.

Nope, I wasn't that way. And I never could be, and as much as I loved her, That wasn't my style and I couldn't live with myself if I had to act that way. I never hit a woman in my life, and Sue would not become the first.

I REMEMBER EARLY in our relationship, on a Friday evening, (I would pick Wuz up at a shopping center near her home every Friday, which was her payday at one of the few jobs she worked, and she had to cash her check) and Sue and I were sitting down over a cup of coffee, in a restaurant at Karls Silver Club in Sparks, NV. a sister City to Reno. We had just cashed a ticket on a $48.00 horse that I had gotten a tip on. Sue turned to me and out of the blue asked: "Can an Episcopalian marry a Jew in Church?" She didn't know it at the time, but she was raised a Methodist.

I told Sue that if she would marry me, I'd convert to any religion she'd like, just to be with her, and in a heartbeat. She quickly said "Oh, I wasn't talking about you and me. I was thinking about someone else". Since we were the only two people sitting there, and I was the only male Jew that she was friendly with, I knew better. And the strange thing was that she was cold sober at the time she asked this.

But that was to be the only time she showed an interest in a permanent relationship with me, except of course as friends. And because I enjoyed her company and didn't want to risk losing it, I tried unsuccessfully to never push the marriage issue. Ultimately it all worked out for the best.

NOT THAT SUE WAS AN ANGEL, she wasn't, but she was my angel. She would not be opposed to a one-night (or longer) stand when she was separated from her husband Don, and waiting for the divorce that Jim had talked her into getting. And those one-night stands she rarely would spend were with me, at least at first. Sex was one thing, but we sleeping together seemed to signify a commitment in her way of looking at things.

Jim was married and had promised Wuz that he would get a divorce and marry her, which is what she told me that she really wanted. Instead he knocked up a younger gal and had to marry her (he did have some redeeming moral values). So much for faithfulness to Sue, or the lack of, from both sides.

Wuz told me that Jim had once wanted to take her to a swingers party, but she backed out as they approached the house, and told him that if he wanted to see her with another man, she was sure I would gladly accommodate (the third slot) his whims, and I certainly would have. But knowing our feelings towards each other, Jim turned it down.

Woozel, Boxing and Me

FOR THE RECORD I didn't jump in the sack with Wuz until Jan. 17, 1983, my 41st birthday. And it was by far the best and yet the weirdest birthday present that I ever had. Knowing Sue, why should I have expected less?

That was to prove a very interesting night. Sue and I we're drinking and laughing, celebrating the event in the coffee shop at the Silver Club, when Jim, who was always spying and checking up on her, found us. Not that our 'place' was any secret. I don't know why Wuzzel seemed to always be attracted to the possessive, jealous guys. Although she once told me that she felt that being jealous proved that someone cared. It was typical Woozel logic.

Jim had tried to call her earlier, and when he found out that she wasn't at home he obviously had a pretty good idea where she would be, still hanging out at the Silver Club with me. Jim drove to the casino to check on her. Her loud laughter pointed the way directly to our booth.

After a few drinks, at my expense of course, Jim arose and said that he was leaving and told Sue to grab her coat, as she was going to be leaving with him. Wuz told him she was having too much fun and that she was going to stay and celebrate with me for a while longer. Jim, of course, got highly insulted and left in a huff. If Sue cared, it certainly didn't show at that point.

Later, although absolutely unplanned, we retired to my room at the casino's hotel (I was divorced and doing public relations for the Silver Club in exchange for the room), and although I know that we 'got it on', I sadly remember none of the details, as we both had really been drinking hard that evening. Drinking that much wound up being something I've regretted to this day. More than having drank too much and to me even far more important, I sincerely regret not remembering much of the first time I had sex with Sue.

My mind was in a heavy fog and I never thought about telling the hotel operator, 'no phone calls', or unplugging the phone from the wall jack, which I saw no reason to do. In the middle of the night the phone rang and Sue jumped up and absolutely freaked out. "Oh my God, it's Jim. He found me. Jim knows that I'm here with you. What should I do now? I got to go. Don't answer the phone". Sue leaped out of bed quickly and began to get dressed. I was taken aback as I certainly didn't expect this reaction from an adult woman.

I didn't care who was calling, I was going to answer the phone, and when I did, I told her jealous 'boyfriend' that he had woken me up, which he did, and that I didn't appreciate it, and although I had no idea where Sue was now, she has left the Silver Club hours ago and was probably at home fast asleep.

He apologized and told me that he was 'worried about her' because he had checked out her house (big surprise) and that her car wasn't there, so she had never come home. I suggested to Jim that Wuz probably had too much to drink and had taken a cab to her house. I don't know if he bought the story or not. I was just trying to get Sue off the hook with him.

I'll never understand how Sue or anyone else could ever get involved with someone like that, who would constantly be checking up on her, (she said the jealousy only proved that he was worried and cared about her). I was surprised to find out later that he was one of the better choices that she would make in her relationships with other men.

AS FOR ME, I had split with my Eileen in the Summer the previous year, and was in the process of going through a divorce, and had absolutely no interest in any other women, except Sue, who I was now hooked on big time.

My ex was pretty upset because after we split up, Sue had taken my side, and much preferred my companionship to hers, and that wasn't going to change no matter how much Eileen would continue to bad mouth me to Sue, and that grew old in a hurry and Wuz would pretty much lose contact with her.

I never told or even suggested to Sue to stop being friends with Eileen. I would never tell anyone how to live their lives, it's not my style. Everyone should make their own decisions in life. Choosing me over my ex was solely Sue's choice, and she made it completely on her own.

AS IT TURNED OUT, some years later, Jim had 'borrowed' some money from the safe at JC Penneys for booze and bills, and although he wanted to, wasn't able to return it. He was forced to resign or face criminal charges. Sue was kind enough to repay the 'loan' out of her meager savings, a loan which he never repaid to her as well.

Sadly, Jim went further downhill quickly from there, eventually returning to his boyhood home in Wisconsin, where, while painting his roof, drunk, he fell off a ladder, cracked his head, and never regained consciousness.

Sue felt bad and somewhat guilty about that for a short time, as she had started seeing Joe who was very possessive, and who, compared to Jim, was a huge step down for her, like a journey into Hell.

IN TRUTH, SHE had told Jim that she was now seeing Joe, and that it was over between them, and remaining in Reno would only equate to easy access to free alcohol for him, and it was best if he returned home. So, with his later demise, I guess the guilt she felt was understandable.

I had a few run-ins with Jim over the years, but he was smart enough to never get confrontational with me. He knew (it was obvious) that I had a thing for Sue and that she was more than just a little fond of me as well. In fact, when he was forced to leave his job, and he had no place to live, and Sue 'innocently' suggested they both move in to my studio apartment. She told Jim that we all could have fun every night on my convertible sofa, which was the only bed in the room.

While he liked the idea of swinging with her (she didn't, except with me, and it would have meant, for an unemployed Jim, free rent and food, as the third party, and that never happened either), he simply didn't want her to be with me because of our strong feelings towards each other, so that idea went by the wayside quickly and he moved into an old trailer with another alcoholic.

There was also a time when Sue called to tell me that 'Jim knows all about us, he's angry and he's coming over to talk to you about it. Whatever you do, don't answer the door'. I laughed at that suggestion and instead left the door wide open. And when, to my surprise, Jim did come over he suggested that we go for a little walk. It was a nice summer afternoon and I agreed. There were no angry exchanges between us, and he was not one bit aggressive, fortunately for him.

In any case, he said the bottom line was "It's up to Sue, if she really wants to be with you, I won't stand in her way". And I told him that I felt exactly the same way, the difference was that while he was checking me out, I meant it. But of course it was nothing more than sort of game Jim and Sue were trying to play with my emotions, and she wound up having dinner and spending that night with him.

There was another time when Wuz came by my studio in the early morning, and told me that Jim was going to commit suicide, and showed me a scribbled note that he had written. Sue understood that I wasn't the jealous type and would be willing to assist her in any situation.

It was just starting getting to become daybreak, but I quickly got dressed, jumped into my car and drove with her to the trailer where Jim was living, which stunk badly from cigarette smoke and alcohol, with empty bottles and full ashtrays strewn everywhere.

Jim was lying on the couch, seemingly in pretty bad shape, but I lifted him up, and along with Sue's help, put him into my car and drove him to the local VA Hospital. He started to sober up and wander around a bit. I was waiting to get him admitted, and Wuz was very concerned that he'd bolt and try to leave. I laughed because I knew I was much bigger and stronger then Jim and that he'd have to get by me first, which, because of my younger day football experience wasn't going to ever happen. I could throw a cross body block as good as anyone around. He

Woozel, Boxing and Me

obviously understood that as well and made no move to run. Besides, I had the car keys.

When Jim got fired from JC Penney, Sue lost her job also, as the new manager knew about her relationship with Jim, which company policy frowned upon. Wuz was told by Jim (probably true) that her days at Penney's were numbered. She quit her job before she was fired. Since Jim no longer worked there, who knew if that was the real reason? Sue didn't enjoy working more than she absolutely had too, and we certainly shared that trait. In truth, I enjoy working for myself, but that's about it. I've always been too damn independent to take any crap from anyone else.

I put Wuz to work for me, to run the office of Ring Arts Magazine, a forerunner of Ring Sports Magazine and Ringsports.com. At her work Sue did little else then sit on her pretty butt and polish and file her nails (which she would bite off anyhow, as well as her toenails) and talk to her friends on the telephone.

But having her there was a good way to keep her away from the bars and Jim, who was out of work also at the time and in the drunk tank more often then not. Jim really didn't seem like a bad guy when he was sober, but those days were now growing few and far between.

AS A RECEPTIONIST, Sue left something to be desired, like everything! For example, forgetting to give me important (or any) messages. I remember one very cold, wet, wintry day when I went out to meet with someone from the boxing community to try to sell them an ad. My car had no heater at that time, and after freezing my ass off for a few hours I returned to the office to see Sue doing her nails (what else?). She seemed surprised: "Oh, I guess that I forgot to tell you. Those people you were supposed to meet called the other day and had to cancel the meeting. They'll call again for another date".

There was another day at the office, which had little to no foot traffic, and I had my hands inside Sue's blouse, fondling her firm breasts, when in walks Alice, the mother of one of Sue's ex-boyfriends, wanting to get them together again. Speaking of being unconscious, I couldn't believe that she didn't notice anything and babbled to Wuz for about a half hour about getting back with her son, (also a druggie, I was told, but much younger than Sue) before finally leaving. But then again, it speaks volumes for the mentality, or lack of, of some of her ex-boyfriends. I'll never know what attracted her to them, although the reverse was all too obvious. She was a real beauty with a great personality and sense of humor.

I CLEARLY REMEMBER one particular day that Sue and I had been drinking at Karl's in Sparks, NV. I only had a few shots of Scotch as I knew I would have to drive her home, and when I'm driving it's only 1-2 drinks. But Wuz had been drinking a lot and I'd venture to say that if you would have lit a match under her mouth, she could have lit up like a gas tank explosion or the Fourth of July fireworks.

It was still daylight when we left to go home, and as we walked out, a beat up looking homeless guy approached us. Wuz often would call these homeless folks 'crusty butts'. "I won't lie to you he said. I'm an alcoholic", he said. "I need a few bucks to buy a drink". Sue for whatever the reason got right into his face. "You certainly do not need a drink right now! I can tell that you've had more then enough already. If you wanted some money for food, fine, I'd give it to you (and she would have) But not one penny for a drink! That's a disgusting habit".

I couldn't believe what I was hearing and I guess the hapless drunk couldn't either, because he had to smell the alcohol on her breath. He just shook his head and walked away talking to himself, while I cracked up, laughing. Sue turned and asked me what I was laughing about and when I told her, she began laughing as well.***

Woozel, Boxing and Me

WUZ WAS OFTEN vain to a fault. I recall on more than one occasion, she almost got a ticket and/or into an accident, because, although she was a very good driver, wouldn't wear the right prescription glasses because they 'didn't match her outfit'. And without the right glasses she was as blind as a bat.***

In 1998, when she learned that she had colon cancer and was getting very weak from the radiation, and had requested cremation after her passing, Wuz kept up her vanity. She decided that she wanting to spend her money to have false eyebrows tattooed on her, as her family tended to have very thin eyebrows, and Sue had inherited the genes.***

I CERTAINLY WAS no angel. When Sue and I got into an argument early in our relationship, and she said that she believed some stupid lie that someone had told her about me. (She later told me that she really did believe me, but was busting my balls) We both had a bit more to drink then we should have. I was upset, and crying a bit, and I got out of her car and told her that it was all over between us and that I never wanted to see her again. I am not a liar and I didn't want anyone, let alone the woman I had come to love, questioning my honesty.

That night I became so depressed, that I mixed alcohol with sleeping pills, and although I can't recall all of the details, I wound up at the restaurant at the Comstock Casino, and while eating there, my face fell into a plate of mashed potatoes and gravy, badly splattering my clothes.

When I woke up the next morning, I was in a friend's house. I know I must have looked a sight. But all it really said was how much I loved Sue and wanted her with me, always. For the record, Wuz came over the next day and acted as if nothing had ever happened. Although she was laughing her ass of when I told her the Comstock story.***

SUE AND I DROVE the 450 plus miles to Vegas and back on many occasions. On the way South we would stop at all the

The Insanity Begins

bars we could find in the small towns (speed traps). There are very few Cities, let alone taverns directly on the main drag, 395 South. We got to know most of the regular bartenders and exchanged new jokes, quenched our thirst (never more then one when driving), and moved on down the road to the next tavern and town for a little more of the same.

We would always make it a point to stop at the Mizpah Hotel in Tonopah for the night, both going and returning from Reno. It was the half-way point of our trip, and a must stop-over, for a good nights sleep and some fun.

It was at the Mizpah one morning, after a Vegas fight, on a return trip to Reno, Sue went down to get something out of my car. She tried to start it, but it wouldn't turn over. She returned to our hotel room saying that try as she might, she just couldn't get it started. I thought that she was kidding me, or that she had done, or was doing something goofy again, but this time she was proven absolutely correct, and it turned out that I was the one who had done something goofy/stupid.

After a few needed repairs in Tonopah, (I had forgotten to change the oil for a year or so) we hit the road again and made it back to Reno where, shortly thereafter, the motor seized. Hey, I'm a writer, not an auto mechanic.

It was at one of these regular return stops at the Mizpah that Sue had me carry *all* of her bags to the room (she needed some make-up or something minor for the morning, and of course that particular item was buried in the last bag I picked up, (that was long before my back went out on me). I made three trips with her luggage and a guy sitting alone at the bar looked up at me, and offered to buy me a drink. He shook his head and said sarcastically "I'll bet you need a drink right now, or are you guys just moving in?" I didn't bother to explain the reason to him, but for the record, I taught Sue how to pack lightly after that.

Finally, when Sue's entire stash of luggage was unloaded in the hotel room, she told me that she needed a drink. So I went down to the bar and ordered her usual, Jack Daniels on the rocks. The guy that I had seen earlier was still sitting there and he just shook his head. "You mean that's for her also?" I said 'yeah, she's really got me pussy whipped'. He laughed, 'Boy, she must really be something special'. She was! It really wasn't that I was pussy whipped, it was simply that I was crazy about her, and would cater to her every whim, and Wuz knew it all to well and had no problem taking full advantage of this.

When I returned to the room, she was nowhere to be found. Sue called out from the bathroom and asked me to bring the drink to her while she was luxuriating in a hot bath, of course with bath oil. While I wasn't a slave to her, I was a slave to love, but I eventually out-grew that also, as the adoration would evolve into something far deeper and beautiful.

KEEP IN MIND this was at least three years before I met my wife to be, Lois. I was young and healthy, single and sexually active, although only with Wuz. Thinking back, I wish I could be just 25% of that now. Unfortunately, the heart and other medications I have to take have made that mission impossible.

WUZ WAS ALWAYS playing practical jokes on me. Early in our relationship, in Las Vegas, before we hit the road for home, I had to stop by a bank to get some extra funds for the three and a half hour drive to Tonopah. Sue spotted a super market in the same parking lot as my bank, and said that while I was in the bank, she'd buy some food and make some sandwiches for us to eat, and save us some money on eating out, on the return trip home.

I really should have known better as Sue (like myself) loved to eat out and would never buy food or make sandwiches, unless she absolutely had to. What did I know? Obviously not very much. I returned to the car, where Sue was sitting back and smiling.

I started the car to hit the road and took a bite out of the 'delicious' sandwich, she handed to me. Tears came to my eyes

The Insanity Begins

and I almost drove off the road. Wuz had loaded it up with Jalapeno peppers. Which I do enjoy, but certainly not hidden in my sandwiches when I'm not expecting them. She just laughed her ass off, while I said a few choice words about her sick sense of humor, under my breath of course.

In more recent years, after I married, on another occasion she put a hard boiled egg under the passenger seat of my car. It was in the summertime and the smell made the word 'ripe' seem mild by comparison. When my wife Lois and I found the egg, after a few days of gagging, I told Sue about it, and she just burst out laughing. I told her we didn't think it was very funny. When she calmed down she admitted her guilt in the fiendish one-woman plot.

SUE ALWAYS HAD a lot of expressions that she picked up and used frequently until she grew tired of them. At this point of her life, her favorite was 'Jesus Christ and General Jackson'. Probably a product of her Southern upbringing.

Another frequently used expression in later years was "Want to buy a deck of cards? It's a good deal." She used that one ad nausem as well.

JEALOUSY WAS NEVER very much of an issue with me. Yes, I wanted Sue with me, and I admit to being a bit upset when she wasn't, but I never really was jealous of anyone and I certainly was not possessive. I always figured that if someone wanted to be with you, they'd be with you, and although our relationship was almost always great, she either didn't always choose to be with me, either as a friend or as my mate, or, she was running around with Jim or Joe, who both dominated her life for a short time, and it was Joe who almost took that life away.

AFTER JOE WENT to jail, for beating up another girlfriend, (Sue had finally wised up and broken up with him well before that), Sue married an older guy, a Chinese, from the Philippines named Jack, so she could get some money and a car and he could become an American citizen. Jack may have been old, but he really cared for Sue and took care of her till her death. Jack was a very hard worker who didn't believe in divorce, although Sue never asked for one. They were married for more than ten years and actually lived together most of that time. I wound up being one of the witnesses for their wedding. In fact, it was Jack's insurance that helped Wuz get quality medical help during her last years.

WHEN WUZ FIRST married Jack, he was living near me, by the Greyhound bus station in downtown Reno, and while she'd visit there often, she never actually lived there with him, although when he eventually moved to a different place, they did live together. It was just a great deal for Sue and companionship for Jack.

I lived in the same housing complex, near Jack, and would see Sue often. I gave Wuz the key to my studio, and even when I wasn't home, she'd stop by and leave me some food and the local newspaper, that I would read almost exclusively for the sports, but wouldn't waste any much needed (at that time) money on buying the rag.

The apartment complex was not well maintained, and it was loaded with roaches. One day Sue asked Jack if he also had roaches in his studio apartment. His response was simple. "Why not?"

On another occasion Sue was with me, having a little fun in the apartment where Jack was living (he was at work) and the super also lived on the same floor, but at the other end of the landing. Jack had previously mentioned to Sue that he had a leak in his bathroom sink faucet. So this time Sue decided that she'd help Jack by confronting the super with the need for repairs.

I not to strongly suggested that she should just mind her own business, because I instinctively realized that this would

The Insanity Begins

be an exercise in futility. I didn't push the issue, because I figured that Wuz couldn't do very much damage. As usual, with Sue, I couldn't have been more wrong. So off she went to ask the super to make the repair.

A few minutes later, I heard loud shouting, and quickly pulling on my pants, opened the front door to see what was going on. Sue was coming towards me and the super, yelling about something which sounded very unpleasant, was following right behind her. As soon as he saw me he stopped dead in his tracks (and wisely so). "What are you doing here?" he asked. "Oh, I know what you're doing here!" I told him he was a fucking genius and if he didn't go back to his broom closet I'd throw him off the balcony (and I would have).

The super immediately realized that I wasn't bluffing. I was much younger, bigger and stronger then he was, and I had a short fuse, particularly when it came to Sue. He wisely returned to his apartment, yelling to me that Sue and Jack would have three days to get out. He obviously didn't have the balls to tell me that I'd have to move also, which, looking back, at that point in time, this was also a very wise move on his part. He wasn't that bright, but he wasn't stupid either.

In any event, when poor Jack came home from work, Sue said to him "I have some good news and some bad news for you". Jack looked at her innocently enough as she continued. "The good news is that your bathroom faucet is going to be fixed". Jack smiled at that. "The bad news is that you're going to be evicted, and you have three days to move".

Surprisingly, Jack didn't seem to get very upset with the news. If he did he certainly never showed it. He simply went out and spoke for a few minutes with the super, and I can only assume that after crossing his palm with gold and silver, and his first born, he came back to the apartment and announced that everything was now taken care of and he would not have to move.

Sue also made friends with an older, alcoholic couple who lived downstairs, in the same complex,, and for a while she was spending more time with them then she did with me.

Birds of a feather, I guess. It hurt because I always saw her car parked downstairs. If I didn't see it, it probably wouldn't have bothered me as much. I didn't dislike these people, but like so may other of her 'friends' they were so far beneath her, that it just made no sense to me. Still, that was her choice and I never mentioned it to her.

Then, one day, without bothering to tell me, Wuz went with them to San Francisco for a few days, and took along some even 'lesser' light, another alcoholic that they had fixed her up with. It kind of pissed me off that I wasn't asked instead, but for some reason, which I still don't understand, at that time Sue had started acting pretty cold towards me. She remained standoffish for awhile, even when she returned, although Wuz said that she had a great time, she acknowledged that this crew had no problem driving her car over potholes and other obstacles. I was a bit hurt since I loved the race-track, which was their destination of choice in the Bay Area, so I wasn't exactly a happy camper.

IT WAS DURING this time that I started getting headaches and dizziness, and was diagnosed with an acoustic neuroma, a tumor on the hearing nerve of my left ear. And while not life threatening (as of now), it's a very slow growing tumor that causes deafness in the ear. Even now I have to go for MRI's for that on an 18 – 24 month basis. If the tumor starts to grow and spreads closer to the brain it will require surgery, and, at age 64, don't have the time or patience for that. Like most other medical problems, it's just something that I intend to out-live.

And my suddenly questionable health took yet another turn for the worst in 1993, when I was somewhat active (hard for me to ever be active now, or then as I recall). I had just finished playing a long game of tennis in the mid-summer heat, when I returned home and found out that I was eligible for something called an executive physical, through my wife Lois's work.

The Insanity Begins

I MET LOIS in 1989, answering her ad in the local paper, and married her in 1990, and it was the best thing I have ever done. Sue wasn't jealous, or at least said that she wasn't. And Lois and I had the understanding that my friends will remain my friends, just as her friends would remain her friends. I didn't want to lose Sue's companionship and goofiness. Laughter had become an integral part of my life.

Actually it was not quite the right information that Lois had gotten on the physical, as it turned out. The fact was that I would get the extensive exam for free, but *only* if they found a medical condition that I was covered for. If I was in good health, which I thought I was at that time, the physical would have cost us some good and much needed money.

Anyhow Saint Mary's hospital performed many tests including one called a heart calcification study, (they say they don't do this test anymore because it's been proven *'unreliable'*. Huh?) this showed I had five arteries 90% or more, blocked. I hadn't noticed any symptoms, but then again, I never paid a lot of attention to my body anyhow. The doctor said if I didn't have bypass surgery, I wouldn't be around till the end of the year, and that was in September. Hell of a rude awakening.

Until I reached my 50th birthday, I was always pretty healthy, or thought that I was. There were a few nagging football/sports related injures, the acoustic neuroma, and that was it. Granted, my diet was far from the best, but who knew? Certainly not me!

I told Sue, who, that day went to the hospital with me, as Lois was at work, that I would be needing the surgery, she went outside the twin hospital doors and threw up. She hated hospitals, probably because of the memories of her father, and didn't even visit me when I had the five bypasses that September. But she would come around often and pick me up for health-needed walks after I returned home.

`Her mother, Amelia, who used to be a nurse told Wuz that I wouldn't be around much longer, which may have been another reason she was unable or didn't want to see me in the hospital.

SO IT WAS an ironic twist of fate that Sue was to spend much of the final years of her life going to doctors and in and out of hospitals, between her colon cancer and her mothers failing health.

I knew that I had to take care of this possibly serious health business as well as running the magazine (Ring Sports), and although the doctor said I'd miss getting out an issue of the magazine (Monthly), I knew that I wouldn't (and didn't, thanks to the efforts of my partner Marv Snow and my wife) and I simply said to the doctor "Let's do it". I came out of the surgery fine, as of now. And although I still have to see a cardiologist on a regular basis, I feel okay. Of course I felt fine before the bypasses as well.

Truth be told, this problem is genetic and sooner or later will take my life, unless something else does me in first. Since the bi-passes, I've had two mild heart attacks and a stroke that knocked out half my right retina.

ONE UNANTICIPATED PROBLEM though, was that all the meds have totally killed my once strong sexual desire and I've even been told at times to stop eating spicy food or having a few drinks with friends. I've learned how to deal with being frustrated and live without the normal sexual needs, but I refuse to totally give up the now limited quality of life and give up the spicy foods, and Johnny Walker Black. And for the record, I cannot take any of the sex meds like Viagra because of a medial condition called vaso vagal.

ONE OF THE THINGS Sue and I did *not* have in common was I have always liked to take care of things as soon as they came up, while Sue was a procrastinator, a trait that probably, ultimately cost Wuz her life.

The Insanity Begins

WHEN I CAME OUT of the hospital, Sue came to visit me at home often, and took me to various places, like Virginia Lake or one of the shopping malls, where we would walk together, as walking, the doc informed me, was very important to my recovery. Sue loved to walk, so that wasn't a problem.***

Just a few months before the heart surgery, in early June of 1993, Sue and I were in Vegas, (I rarely ventured to Vegas from mid - May to mid - September) and as expected, it was damn hot. Wuz, who could always out-walk me, got on my case because of my lack of energy, as she was out-walking me, (and although I was short of breath and sweating my ass off, I attributed that to the heat, and certainly not my heart) and Sue told me that I looked 'like death warmed over,' when we ultimately reached our destination. I was a bit short of breath and didn't notice any chest pains although my clothes were drenched with sweat and sticking to me, which I figured was the desert heat and nothing more. Sue had no idea how right that statement she made was, at the time. In truth, the old friends we were visiting with also made a similar remark.

SUE AND I WOULD TAKE numerous two-three hour car trips to Northern California. Most of these jaunts were to Rancho Cordoba, outside of Sacramento, and Modesto/Stockton, where her only son Dorian was either incarcerated or living. We also went to the State Fair in Sacramento on a couple of occasions, although it was always held in the heat of the summer and that limited our enjoyment. The trips were almost always fun and lasted a few days at a time.

WE ALSO MANAGED two trips to San Francisco. During the first, among other things, I took her on a boat ride to Alcatraz Island, which she fell in love with (the Island, not the boat ride), and told me that "this was the most romantic place that I had ever taken her". Huh? A prison was the most romantic place I had taken her to? What did that say about her? What did that say about me?

Sue was intrigued by "The Rock" and wanted to come back the next day, make sandwiches and camp out overnight. It would have been highly illegal, but no matter, we never did it anyhow.

ON THE OTHER TRIP to the City by the Bay, we were staying at a friend's house, in a nearby City. He was gone for the week, and I wanted to go to San Francisco and see an old girl friend, who was married with children (good name for a TV sitcom) and who I had not seen in many years. We got into an argument about that, (Sue told me some time later that she was jealous, but that she'd never admit it to anyone else). The argument grew heated and got to the point where I got very angry and very careless, and turning the car around, I cut off a few cars in getting back to the bridge to return to the place we were staying.

As a direct result of that anger I got off at the wrong exit, and wound up in a largely industrial community, Emoryville. It was a Sunday morning and the City was very quiet. While I was stopped by a red light, Sue witnessed an altercation in an empty parking lot, where a black man was yelling at a black woman in a parked car, and we both heard a baby in the woman's car, crying. Suddenly a lug wrench appeared in his hand and he was swinging it at her car.

Unfortunately, these were the days before cell phones, so what would happen next could not be easily avoided. Sue asked me (it sounded more like a demand) to stop the car and I told her no, and that she should mind her own damn business, that we'd call the cops as soon as we could find a payphone.

Sue saw a pay phone in the lot, or said that she did, and like an idiot I believed her, and pulling my car over, let her get out to call the police. Of course there was no pay phone on the lot. Just a beat up abandoned building and a boarded up bar and

The Insanity Begins

the two, now three, cars. The next thing I knew I heard Sue screaming loudly "Hey Buddy, leave her alone!"

Never known for my great speed, I jumped out of the car and got to her just as the guy with the lug wrench had turned, and it looked for all the world like he was going to swing it at her. I pushed Sue out of the way, although I was also defenseless, and told her to get the hell out of there and call the cops.

Of course she didn't listen, listening would have been way out of character for Wuz. She stubbornly stood right her grounds. And the black guy turned angrily towards me, and I firmly believe that he was about to swing the lug wrench in my direction, when, just like in the western movies, the good guys, the Emoryville Police, in their white patrol cars, pulled up and disarmed the assailant at gunpoint. Someone else obviously had seen what was going on and had the good sense to dial 911, and I thank God for that.

WUZ GOT BACK into the car and we drove off, and she quickly asked me to stop at a bar we were passing, where a lot of well dressed Black Muslims were standing around outside, as she wanted to get a cold beer. I told her she can have all the beer she wanted when we returned to the house, or at least got out of the immediate area. It was one of the few times in our entire relationship that I actually told her 'no'.

I also scolded Wuz and told her that it was a very brave, but also a very foolish thing that she had just done. She just looked at me, shrugged her shoulders and casually said "Well, maybe it was stupid, but you came after me, so how smart do you think you are?" I tried to explain the difference, which was that I just happened to be in love with her, but somehow, even to this day, I was never sure that the explanation ever completely sunk in.

WHEN WE RETURNED home and Sue told her family of the experience, her mom, agreeing with me, said that it was really very stupid of her, but her older sister Marian told me that she would have done exactly the same thing. Guess living dangerously can be a family trait.

I suppose that all the action of that morning in Emoryville had really turned Sue on, because when we returned to the house, we had the best sex that we had up till that point, in our relationship.

THINKING BACK, SUE would rarely tell me that she loved me, but the words were never really necessary, we had a much stronger bond that had grown between us then just love, and the words never had to be said, as we both knew it.

That however also changed a bit towards the end of her life, when knowing that it was almost over, Wuz did say that she loved me a lot more often. In fact, although we always used to sleep in separate beds, when available, the last month or two she asked me to just lie down next to her and hold her all night. It was quite an understandable request under the circumstances.

ONE TIME, NEAR THE END, Wuz told me that I 'was her hero', but if I ever told anyone she said that, she would d deny it. I'm still not quite sure what that was all about.

ON ANOTHER OCCASION Sue and I were given a free room at the old Aladdin Hotel, when we were in Las Vegas to cover a fight. Wuz went to the ladies room while I waited for her by the gift shop located just across the hall from it. Sue walked out, with two elderly, heavy set, grey hair ladies behind her, and Wuz let out one of the loudest and smelliest farts I can ever recall. In fact, one of the ladies actually jumped back. Sue just kept on going, as if nothing happened. I turned my back on the scene, laughing and pretended that I didn't know her, at least until they left and I was able to stop laughing.

The Insanity Begins

THEN THERE WAS the time that Wuz and I were eating dinner at the Bally's 'Big Kitchen' Buffet in Las Vegas. She had taken along some type of tape recorder that said in a high pitched voice four negative comments, like f--k you, or you're an asshole. There were two wealthy (you could tell by their fur stoles and jewelry) elderly ladies at the next table, and Sue just couldn't resist. Suddenly comes blaring forth "You're an asshole, You're an asshole". The ladies jumped in surprise, and then in our natural voices we turned towards them, and asked, 'did you hear that'? Of course they denied it, but it was good for plenty of laughs in the evening conversation. Wuz and I always played off each other very well.

THERE ARE PLENTY of other memories and "Woozel Bwain" as I called Sue, stories, which will be related in subsequent chapters.

Round II
Boxing bits and pieces.

FIRST, A COUPLE of humorous non-boxing memories that I recall happening during my long lifespan.

IN 1979, WHEN I was running for a seat on the Reno City Council, I was invited to a get together with some young voters at a Fraternity house at the University of Nevada – Reno. My ex-wife, Eileen, who was prematurely grey, was by my side, (we were not yet separated) when a pretty young lass came up to me and said "You're Rusty Rubin? You know I never made it with a politician before". Taken aback, I looked at Eileen, who was at a loss for words, then back at the young gal, and simply said "You know, I never made it with a politician before either".

ANOTHER TIME, WHEN I was having severe back problems and was put into a body cast. I was running for State Assembly, knocking on doors in a rural area, north of Reno, when Eileen started honking the horn.

I was at the door to this fenced home, and no one had answered and, as I slowly walked back (lots of puddles as it had rained earlier in the day), my wife, Eileen, started yelling something and waving at me. I turned around to see a bull, pawing the ground, getting ready to charge.

Although never known for my speed, I took off like a bat out of hell, and slid under the fence, and right into a mud puddle, feeling the bad breath of the bull on the back of my neck. That was one voter that I didn't reach, and obviously was a strong supporter of my opponent, and that is not a political bullshit story.

MY WIFE LOIS and I were in Kentucky for the Derby, which I was covering for another publication. The event fit into my schedule and sounded like a nice working vacation, which it was. The weather was great, except for a bit of rain on Derby day, and I found that both Louisville and Lexington have lots to see and are great Cities to visit. This is before the Muhammad Ali Cultural Center was built and before a street in Louisville was named after him.

One of the places we visited while in Kentucky was the Makers Mark (bourbon) brewery, which Lois thought smelled fantastic. So after the guided tour, she decided to go out and buy a bottle of the beverage, for us to enjoy. We stopped at a small general store for the purchase. Lois went in but came back empty handed and looking confused. "I can't buy the bourbon here," she sadly proclaimed. When I asked her why, she shrugged her shoulder and said "I guess it doesn't rain enough here. The guy said we were in a *dry* county".

GROWING UP IN Brooklyn, my best friend at the time, Harvey, and I worked in a pharmacy. One day Harvey made a delivery to a nearby hospital. He came back with green scrubs and a stethoscope that he had confiscated under his jacket, with every intention to return it, after we could figure out a way do some harmless mischief. And a few days later, it was returned.

Late that afternoon some of the guys were just hanging out in our basement clubhouse. When I arrived there from my home. I had just gotten a call from a friend, who gave me a hot tip for the first race, the first half of the daily double at Roosevelt Raceway, which was located on Meadowbrook Parkway in Westbury, Long Island (now a shopping center), about a one-hour drive from Brooklyn. We quickly jumped into my car and had to really speed to make the opening race. In fact, I was exceeding the speed limit by quite a bit.

Suddenly a highway patrol car pulls alongside us with siren and lights going, and Harvey leans out the window, still wearing the uniform and stethoscope, and yells "I have an emergency operation at Meadowbrook Hospital." Instead of a well deserved speeding ticket we wound up with a police escort, lights, siren and all, to the hospital which was about ten minutes away from the racetrack. We made it with time to spare and the horse won.

WE'VE ALL SEEN our share of bad decisions in boxing. The most disgraceful that I can recall was the verdict in the Holyfield - Lewis I heavyweight title fight, held at Madison Square Garden in NYC on March 11, 1999.

The fight was clearly won by Lewis. In fact, if Holyfield legitimately took three rounds in the 12-round fight, I'd be very surprised. If any of the other rounds were close enough to question, I'd be shocked. Yet, with the help of a couple of poor scorings by the judges, Holyfield was given a draw. One judge, in fact, had Lewis <u>only winning three rounds</u>. The fact that one of the other judges scored it for Lewis and another judge a draw, which made little sense as well, didn't look good for the image of what many folks have come to consider a gutter sport.

Of course the other judge, who scored it a draw, had the fight much closer than the off-base judge did, but was still obviously wrong in the scoring as well, which he freely admitted to, later on. These kind of ridiculous decisions go a long way in arousing suspicions and giving the sport of boxing a bad name.

I RECALL SITTING at the second floor bar in the Comstock Hotel Casino in Reno, on June 6, 1987, with Sue, watching the Greg Haugen/Vinny Pazienza I, lightweight title fight, in Providence, R.I. Talk about your bad hometown decisions.

It wasn't the fact that we had lost a small wager, as much as the extent to which the boisterous crowd was able to influence the judges scoring. Greg Haugen had little facial damage, because few big punches landed on it, and Paz came out of the fight looking like he was put through a meat grinder. When the unanimous decision for Pazienza was announced we were still totally sober and <u>still</u> almost fell off our bar stools.

To this day, I rib my good friend, and outstanding fight judge (except for this one, he's human) Keith McDonald about it. He still thinks that he scored it right. I know that he's totally honest, so go figure.

Sue had made a wager of fifty bucks with her brother in law at the time, that Haugen would win the fight. As a gesture of protest and humor combined, Sue took a $50 bill, blacked out the eyes of Ben Franklin and wrote "blind judge" on the bottom of the picture on the bill, before putting it in her sister's curbside mailbox.

But to say a fight has been corrupted because a judge is either inept, as in the first case, or perhaps influenced by the crowd, as in the other, is simply something that has not and cannot be proven. There is absolutely no doubt in my mind that it's very hard to block out the crowd noises when scoring a fight, and at times, it can be an almost impossible task. Being a fight judge is thankless, and makes me glad that I'm not a boxing judge.

TYPO'S OCCUR IN all publications at one time or another, and in Ring Sports, there would be no exception. As long as the word that is typed is legit, the computer's spell/grammar check won't pick it up, and when we are under a tight deadline, we rarely would find enough time to grammar check an article that has been submitted to us at the last minute.

And so it happened that in an article about an Oscar de la Hoya fight, our late writer Shirley Norman wrote: "In his excitement De la Hoya "jumped" on the ring post. Sadly the "J" in jumped was misread by the scanner, as a "D", and read that Oscar had an accident and did a no-no on the corner post.

On another occasion, sportswriter and friend Mike Houser was opining about women's boxing, writing that "men are physically superior to women." It was my fault here, because somehow it came out "men are physically supper to women." A bit kinky, but funny nonetheless, but probably not to those who strongly support equal rights for women.

AND, A NUMBER of years back, one of my writers at the time, Howie Reed, wrote about boxing judge and HBO TV commentator Harold Lederman, calling him Harold. "My shorts are too tight, Lederman" wrote Howie, referring to Harold's very high pitched voice. decided that knowing Harold usually had a great sense of humor, I'd leave the comment in the article.

About ten days after the paper came out, and had reached the East Coast, where Harold resides, I got a call at 4:30 AM, from an angry Lederman in NY saying "I know what time it is in Reno. This is Harold "my shorts are too tight" Lederman, and I really didn't appreciate what Howie Reed wrote in his column.

I felt kind of bad for Harold, but I didn't appreciate the early wake up call, (the home/office phones are on only 8 hours a day now) but after a while I really thought the whole thing was pretty funny, and I still do. Of course when, and if, Harold reads this, I'll be expecting another angry telephone call.

Howie Reed, although I'm sure that he meant well, and donated his consider-able writing talents to Ring Sports, gratis, had unintentionally caused me other problems over the years. He applied for press credentials for himself (a no-no) for the Prince Naseem Hamed - Marco Antonio Barrera fight in April, 2001. It shouldn't have happened, Howie should have known better, but the credentialing folks who approved it should have also, as they approved it without first checking with the editor, me. Our stringent policy had always been that only the editor can put in for credentials.

This brief series of events caused some problems with my wife Lois, who went to Las Vegas with me, to cover the fight, while Wuz watched the house (office). I didn't go to Vegas very often, (don't do heat well) and Lois much less, so I expected much better treatment from the credentialing folks, particularly because I was the managing editor and Lois was the driving force behind the publication and website, and did the layout as well.

But because of the credentialing bodies' laziness in their lack of checking and enforcing, Lois had to sit in the press room (outdoor tent) and I had to sit in terrible, hard, cold metal seats. Lois caught a cold (which I caught afterwards) and my back was very sore from the very hard, uncomfortable seats that provided little to no leg room. I was there to cover a fight, and you can't accurately write about something that you can't see. Another problem here was that there was a lot of folks who didn't belong in front of me (circulation and seniority speaking) or weren't even members of the press and no one in security bothered to check. I was not to become a fan of BZA as a credentialing body.

So I figured that I would make this a one-time problem, and Howie Reeds screw-up would not happen again. So I sent out a memo to all my writers that I alone am, and would be responsible for all West Coast credentials. This was something the credentialing body and writers certainly should have been aware of. I thought this procedure was understood, as the credentialing bodies always send me the application anyway.

BUT IN LATE 2004, I again tried to get passes for Lois and myself for the Barrera - Morales III fight, and the same credentialing body, BZA, said "no spouses." The fact that Lois was the publisher and that we'd have no publication or website without her, meant absolutely nothing to these people, and although there were many empty seats in the press row, as well as the usual people who don't belong, who sneak in, and whom security never checks, BZA remained stubborn.

I cancelled the hotel and plane reservations, and although I was a bit frustrated, I didn't take the complaint further, because I didn't want risking my writers having problems in future fights. Why did I decide to make it an issue for this book? Because it's about time someone had the guts to stand up to these guys who just don't know how to do their job, although I admit it can be a tough one.

Rather than attack the gal at BZA for the screw-ups, I asked a friend to gift wrap a tube of Preparation H, and give it to her(the gal from BZA) for a Christmas present from me, with the words "to my favorite hemorrhoid." He didn't take me serious, although I was at the time.

I CERTAINLY HAVE NOT been the only one put off by the actions of the credentialing bodies, (other members of the press have had problems with BZA as well) so I didn't take it personally. What I did object to is that the good seats at the Barrera - Hamed fight that were rightfully-earned by myself and many other members of the media by circulation and seniority, were given to some people who didn't have our circulation numbers and seniority and some weren't even members of the Press Corps. Of course, the problem of non-credentialed writers sitting with the press could and should have been handled by MGM Grand security, certainly not BZA.

Currently, I get reports that members of the working (boxing) press are at times refused credentials because the credentialing folks allow folks from non-boxing publications to take the spot at ringside.

After the way Lois was slighted, I sent the memo to all my writers after that fight, re-stating that I alone was to assign the credentials on all the West Coast fights. This was made crystal clear to everyone. Howie Reed took it personal, which in fact it was, although I certainly didn't intend to embarrass him by calling him out on it, (why I sent it to the entire staff) and he resigned. I still like the guy and enjoyed his writing style, although if his work was not edited entirely and carefully, some of his articles could have cost me a few major lawsuits.

IN THE LATE 1990's I was at the MGM Grand in Vegas, eating brunch with the late Vegas based writer Jack Welsh and another friend, Phillip, from Reno via San Francisco and Thailand. Our waitress who appeared to be in her mid to late 30's, had a little gut on her. My Thai friend who obviously wasn't acquainted with American customs turned around, gently patted her stomach, and asked "When the baby coming"? Talk about embarrassing moments. Jack and I just looked at each other and quickly back at the menu. We couldn't believe he said that. It was yet another of life's ongoing string of surprising and embarrassing moments.

I RECALL THAT in 1985, four years after I had met Sue and long before I met Lois, I had started a publication called "Ring Arts" and had to sit in the top row at Caesars Palace outdoor arena to watch the Hagler - Hearns legendary fight, and all I could see was the sweat glistening off Marvin Hagler's bald head. Yes, I was at one of the greatest fights of all time, but I didn't get to see it very well. But I certainly wasn't angry, as Ring Arts Magazine was a pretty new publication and hadn't earned the respect it would eventually come to get in the boxing community.

My solution to this particular problem was to write in the next publication: "All that I could see of this great action-packed, three round fight from my vantage point high above the ring, was the sweat glistening off Marvin Hagler's bald head." It was the last time I had problems with the seating at that venue.

I also had problems early on, with another credentialing body, Magna Media, who would continuously give me and my writers terrible seats at the fights they handled. Finally, we were able to communicate, (novel idea for two communications companies) and I found out that my writer, the late Shirley Norman, was not showing up to the fights, but also not calling to tell them she wouldn't be there for whatever reason, which was very unprofessional and a major mistake on her part. She was a veteran journalist and should have known better. Shirley was getting on in years and had been having some serious health problems, but that is still no excuse for not using common courtesy. These incidents with Magna Media turned out to be purely a communication problem which was resolved peacefully, with just one phone call.

I RECALL DOING a talk show on a local radio station in Reno, with outstanding referee Mills Lane and other local boxing folks as guests, and somehow I got tongue tied when Buster Douglas's name came up. I first pronounced it Duster Blublas, and every time I tried to correct it, it got worse and worse, and my guests in the studio were rolling on the floor as I fumbled around, searching for the correct pronunciation, which I finally gave up on. I just looked at them and said "Yeah, easy for you guys to say".

One of the times that I unexpectedly "lucked out" was when Wuz and I were in Las Vegas for a major fight (Hagler - Hearns) with two of my other writers. A day before the event we were going to lunch when we ran into former great champions Gene Fullmer and Carmen Basilio and their wives. We had lunch together and enjoyed more laughs than I ever remember, with or without the food.

It certainly was not a good time to be without my tape recorder, but who knew? It was, however, a lesson well-learned.

Here were two great former world champions in the ring, and they exhibited every bit of class outside of the squared circle as well. Fullmer has been very active with the Rocky Mountain Golden Gloves and Carmen and his current wife Josie are surefire guests at every major charitable and other boxing functions. They are just four of the most beautiful people around and a credit to our sport. We remain friends, and I usually see all of them at the annual World Boxing Hall of Fame induction ceremonies in Southern California.

IN AUGUST, 2000, I was highly honored to receive an invitation to attend my very good friend, the legendary Eddie Futch's, 89th (and sadly final) birthday party in Las Vegas. I don't like Vegas in the summer time, it's way to hot for me, but Eddie was someone special, not just to the sport, but to me personally, and who, along with his lovely wife Eva were longtime friends. So despite a few health problems, like anemia, undiagnosed at the time, I knew that I had to be there. Among the guests on hand were Joe Frazier and Michael Spinks. It was a fun time, but physically, I just wasn't up to taking it all in. I certainly wasn't the life of the party. Fortunately, I wasn't the one being honored, and no one took notice.

I was planning on visiting Vegas in September 2001, for Eddie's 90th birthday, but the tragic events of September 11th put a temporary halt to the party, and as it turned out, sadly, for good. That year Eddie's party was scheduled to be at Caesars Palace and a fundraiser for the non-profit boxing relief organization FIST. I wouldn't have missed it unless I was on my death bed. Eddie and his wonderful wife Eva knew that we couldn't afford it at the time, as we were under very tight financial circumstances. They offered to give is two of his very few free tickets that he was issued for the November event to Lois and myself. Sadly, Eddie passed away in his sleep before the re-scheduled event happened, but I found it necessary to fly to Vegas to be at his funeral and pay him my sincere respects, as well as to comfort his lovely wife. He was a dear friend, Eva still is.

Eddie had told me a few years before his passing, that I was the "classiest person he had ever known." Yes, he was sober. I don't think I ever saw this all-time great trainer indulge in anything stronger than a glass of wine. Coming from anyone else but Eddie, it would not be a great compliment, but coming from Eddie, it was unbelievable. If there was anyone I ever looked up to in this world, let alone in this lifetime, it would be Eddie Futch. He was simply the best.

IN APRIL OF 2001, my brother who lived in New Jersey, sent me an e-mail to pass along, calling for a boycott of Chinese goods in retaliation for the Chinese forcing down one of our spy planes in International waters and holding the plane and its crew hostage. The crew was released about ten days later.

In any event, one of the folks that I e-mailed the message to was George Chung, a top martial artist, then a boxing promoter, and then front man for Top Rank in Northern California. George was a seemingly nice guy and very likable.

George thought the e-mail was *'so funny'* that he e-mailed me back and forwarded it to some others I had sent it to, writing that he was both Korean and Chinese. I guess, from his response, he felt that I was stereotyping him, and that was never even a distant thought in my mind, let alone my intention. I don't stereotype and I don't like prejudice of any kind. I don't see how anyone can be associated with boxing and feel otherwise.

AND SPEAKING OF unusual, the strangest occurrence, in all my years, in and out of boxing took place *before* a fight in New Orleans. The promoter, Bobby Walshak invited Lois and I to be his guest at the event, which although sparsely attended, turned out to be an excellent fight card. (I happen to love Cajun food).

Boxing bits and pieces

I distributed the latest issue of my magazine at the press conference, and among those on hand were Tony Wilson, a former light heavyweight contender from the UK. He had brought with him a friend, Maurice, a muscular kick boxing champion, who had recently retired, and had turned to managing fighters, and Tony's charge was a female fighter, Cheryl Robertson. We had known in advance that Cheryl was to fight on the card, but I had no idea who her manager/trainer was at the time, and even if I did, I wouldn't have put this story together on a bet.

At this time we were running cartoons in the magazine, done by a kindly subscriber in Canada, who had recently sent us about a dozen new ones. My wife Lois randomly selected one that depicted an incident that had actually happened (although we didn't know it at the time) in the UK, depicting a lady, with a handbag, in the ring corner, hitting a fighter standing in the corner, on his head with her purse.

Tony scanned the pages of Ring Sports, looked at the cartoon quietly, looked up and asked, with a somewhat angry expression on his face, what the meaning of the photo was. I told him the truth, and he than quietly explained to me that the lady that the cartoon we used depicted his mother, who had attacked his opponent in the ring in London, with her purse, after Tony had lost what she thought was a bad decision.

Tony also made it a point of telling me that he was sick and tired of being made fun of because of that incident. Fortunately, when we explained what had happened, Tony understood that it was certainly not intentional on our part, and he laughed.

Since then we have become good friends and talk on the phone four or more times a year. However, I'd like to question an actuary of the chance of this happening, with both of us coming from different parts of the World, meeting in New Orleans, the chance pick of the cartoon, etc. Must be pretty high odds, I'll wager (or I should have).

BACK TO MY Cajun food comment, when we were in New Orleans, I asked a waiter in a high class Bourbon Street restaurant what people who are on low fat or low cholesterol diets order when they go out to eat in the Crescent City. Seemed like a logical question since Cajun food is not known to be especially good for one's heart. The waiter thought for a second and replied: "They don't order anything, they starve."

ANOTHER INCIDENT WHERE I almost had to lace up my gloves again, came in 1997, when I was supposed to do an interview with middleweight (at the time) James Toney (spelled with an 'e') at the Clarion (now Atlantis) Hotel/Casino in Reno. It was the 15th birthday party for the hotel with free champagne and cake for all who attended. So, when Sue, who was feeling somewhat depressed at the time, saw all the goodies, she decided not to accompany me on the interview which I was to do in Toney's room. I left Wuz to enjoy herself and told her I'd probably be back in about 15 minutes. I figured that although she seemed depressed about her only child, (son), being incarcerated again, booze or no booze how much damage could she possibly do in 15 minutes. I should have known the answer. If I would have thought about it, I would have insisted (I'm sure to no avail) that she accompany me.

Although he never enjoyed a reputation of being an overly pleasant sort, I was certainly not expecting James Toney to be antagonistic, let alone threatening towards me as I entered the room. I had predicted in my publication, Ring Sports Magazine, that his opponent Mike McCallum would take a close decision from him. Lots of other boxing folks had picked the fight as well, and many had also picked his opponent, the "Body Snatcher." However, I was the only one who picked McCallum that was doing this interview a few days before the fight.

But it was I, not Daniel, who unknowingly and fearlessly walked into the lions den that day, as Toney charged out of his room and started ranting and raving and threatening me, saying: "You are not my fucking friend," because I had picked against him, and many other very choice, not-for-children type words. This was something that had never happened or even occurred to me could happen, in all my years in the fight game. And, it has not happened since.

I certainly didn't want any altercation (he was much younger and in far better shape than I was), but being brought up on the mean streets on the outskirts of Bedford Stuyvesant, I never learned the meaning of backing down, no matter what the odds. And believe me, although Toney, a future heavyweight contender, would be fighting a natural heavyweight in me, he was the very <u>heavy</u> favorite here. Very, very, heavy! Hell, I would have bet my life on him. Come to think of it, I almost did.

Truth be told, the fastest speed I've ever had, even in my football days, was slow at best, so there was nowhere to run, even if I wanted to. So I stepped back, put my hand on a chair that I would have definitely swung at him if he took the first shot, and I waited. If I was going down, I was not going without a fight, albeit an obviously unfair one.

Fortunately, for me I'm sure, Toney's manager at the time, Jackie Kallen, a very nice lady, stepped quickly between us, and we quickly wound up at the downstairs bar, me doing the interview with her instead of James. For the record, Toney did win the fight, but fortunately, not against me. That was obviously a stand-off (no contest) because I'm still around. And, for what it's worth, the next time I ran into James, in Los Angeles a few years later and he was a perfect gentleman (and then a true heavyweight), and the incident has never been brought up again.

When Jackie Kallen went to the downstairs bar with me, over a few drinks, I conducted a nice interview with and about her. I figured if Toney didn't want the publicity, I'd give it to Jackie Kallen, a classy lady involved in what is generally thought of as a man's business.

I thanked her and went to search for Sue, who was not where I left her. About ten minutes later, I finally found Wuz, totally drunk and crying. She was at a different bar than where I had first dropped her, and casino security, when they found out I was with Wuz, asked me (okay, strongly suggested) to take her home. I did, but it was to my home, because she was in no shape to work up the flight of stairs that led to her apartment.

I put her on our king-sized bed to sleep it off, and I called and told Lois, who was at work, that we had a temporary house guest, as Sue was still fast asleep when I left her to pick my wife up.

I don't think Sue ever got out of the bed that night, and Lois and I had to share a cramped, single bed, in another room (which is logically where I should have put Sue in the first place). Wuz was a lot smaller than Lois and I, but as usual Wuz did the unexpected and slept through everything.

SUE HAD THE habit of using the expression "Rusty said" even when I didn't, which was usually the case, and then never bothered to tell me what I 'said'. That got me into some uncomfortable situations at times both with her friends and family and when Wuz was around, and the subject in question came up, I would always get kicked under the table or an 'accidental' elbow to my ribs to go along with the conversation.

I RECALL GOING on a bus tour to Laughlin, when in Vegas, with Sue. The bus had a few mechanical problems and we came back late and missed the fight that we had flown to Vegas to see. I got a call from a Canadian radio station, when we returned to the room. Lois had given them the phone number, which was not usually a problem. The station wanted to talk to me about the fight that we had missed, and I was suddenly placed in a very uncomfortable and potentially embarrassing situation.

"And on the line with us we have Ring Sports Magazine managing editor Rusty Rubin, who has just returned from sitting ringside at the big championship fight in Las Vegas. Rusty, what did you think of the fight? Did it live up to your expectations"?

Fortunately, the bout was between two big hitters with questionable chins, so I was able to improvise. "It was indeed a great fight, for as long as it lasted". I got lucky and called it right on the money, because I had no way of knowing the bouts victor at that point. Sue was beside herself in the next bed, laughing her ass off.

BERNARD FERNANDEZ, WELL respected boxing scribe and then President of the Boxing Writers Association of America, adds these two gems:

In late 1998, Bernard journeyed to Vegas to cover two fights: one between Don Lalonde and Sugar Ray Leonard and another between Thomas Hearns and James "The Heat" Kinchen.

In between the shows, Fernandez gets a last minute call to go to Tucson to cover a fight between Marvis Frazier, who was going to retire after the fight, and journeyman Phil Brown. Because of the two major events the bout was scheduled in between, Bernard found himself in the press section, in the same front row with the only other reporter, the ring girls and the guy who held the ropes for the gals.

As it happened, there was a biker gang/group of about 15, who were in attendance, sitting ringside, and right behind the TV cameraman, who was doing his job, but was also blocking their vision. The bikers screamed and yelled, but to no avail.

In round two, a couple of the bikers went to the concession stand and came back with beer and hot dogs. It wasn't long after that the cameraman was soaked in beer, had mustard in his hair and on his clothes, and there were hot dogs in the ring, and the ring card girls were hiding under the table.

To add to this, Marvis Frazier was constantly hitting low, right in front of the referee, who was allowing the fouls to happen. Finally, those in charge of this venue deemed it wise to have the bikers moved to seats where their vision wasn't obstructed.

All this left Fernandez with a wealth of stuff to use in his copy. When he called his office he was informed, that because of the Philadelphia Eagles football game and other stories, he had only 14 inches of copy to work with. Faced with the choice, Fernandez did his job and just wrote a fight report (Marvis won, then retired) leaving the rest of the story to be told in this book.

FERNANDEZ FONDLY RECALLS the time when Mike Tyson was ruling the heavy-weights and Evander Holyfield the cruisers. Evander was slated to meet James "Quick" Tillis at Caesars Tahoe, in his heavyweight debut.

Tillis had set up a sparring tent outside of Caesars and would work out in public, then sign autographs.

A few days before the fight, Bernard and a radio reporter from a local station asked to do interviews. Beau Williford, Tillie's manager at the time, asked them to wait a half hour and visit him in his room where, when cooled down, he'd be glad to oblige.

He did. What the radio reporter didn't know was that Tillis was from the Tex Cobb school of speaking, where almost every other word out of his mouth was four letters, beginning with "F".

Bernie allowed the radio reporter to go first, so they wouldn't interrupt each other during the interview. Sadly nothing Tillis said was going to be usable for the young man, on public radio, but his final question to "Quick" was "What's the difference between training and the actual fight"? Without skipping a beat, Tillis replied. "Training is just like foreplay, leading up to the main event, 'fucking'." The reporter left without anything usable to report to the shows listeners.

OUTSTANDING RING ANNOUNCER Mark Beiro was working a fight at Lake Tahoe, when he suddenly lost most of his eyesight, due to diabetes. A fellow scribe, Mike Houser, sat next to him, and read him the names of the fighters, and the result of each fight. Fortunately, much of Mark's eyesight returned, although he's having problems again, as of this writing.***

Round III

Ring Humor and More

THESE GEMS WERE sent to me by Angelo Prospero, boxing writer and historian:

IN THE RING, Carmen Basilio was as ferocious and war-like as a Hun. He was signed to fight one Arly Siefer in Louisville in 1959, a prelude to Kentucky Derby week. From the outset, it was clear Siefer was overmatched and outclassed. In round three, he whispered to Basilio in a clinch, "Please carry me Mr. Basilio, you're the better man." Basilio replied, "Say goodnight, kid," and kayoed him with a vicious left hook. One thing about Carmen, he asked no quarter and gave none.

After giving Golden Boy Art Aragon a pounding, stopping him in eight rounds, Basilio met Aragon in the coffee shop the next day. "What's the big idea of giving me such a bad beating, Carmen? You left me brain dead," Aragon playfully remarked. "You don't have a brain or you wouldn't have fought me," Carmen answered. That was Carmen Basilio as irreverent as ever.

ROSS VIRGO, ROCHESTER, NY, welterweight rose from Olympic alternate to number five in the World. He beat Fitzie Pruden, Basilio and Tony Pellone and was scheduled to meet Kid Galivan and Billy Graham in Madison Square Garden. At age 22, he met a beautiful young lady whose family had a few bucks. After a brief engagement and impending marriage, his future-in-laws asked him to quit the ring and offered to set him up in the restaurant business.

While mulling over the offer, Virgo took a fight in his second hometown, New Orleans, against a non-entity, Jack O'Brien. Virgo game him a pasting for four rounds and was doing the same in round five when the crowd gasped. The referee collapsed and died in the ring. They ruled the fight a draw.

Virgo figured that was the sign he needed and retired. He opened the fashionable Dickens Restaurant in Rochester and became one of the city's leading civic and sports personalities.

FRITZIE ZIVIC WAS one of the boxing game's dirtiest fighters. He knew all the illegal tricks of the trade and used them. Only once, did he meet his match. In a bout between hometown rivals, Zivic met the Pittsburgh Kid, Billy Conn.

In round one, Zivic rubbed his laces against Conn's eyes. One thing about the great Billy Conn, he was never intimidated and feared no man. Billy said, "You want to fight that way, Croat, let's go," and ripped a vicious left to the mid-section, about a foot below the belt. Zivic was so stunned at his opponent's tenacity, he fought fair and square the rest of the way and lost a ten-round decision.

JOE LOUIS HAD the ability to say the right thing at the right time. He was matched against Tony Musto in his "Bum of the Month" campaign. Louis stood 6'2" while Musto was tops at 5'8". As the one-sided fight progressed, Musto kept getting lower and lower in his crouch until Louis was hammering at his shoulders and neck. Finally, they stopped the bout. Louis deadpanned afterwards, "I'd never be any good fighting midgets."

WILLIE PEP, WHO won more fights (229) than any pugilist ever, had a love affair with the ring, a sentiment not shared by his father. Papa Pep was the breadwinner of the family when Willie started his clandestine amateur career.

One night, 16 year old Willie couldn't hide the obvious, a cut and a black eye. He did convert his watch and trophies won into fifty dollars cash. When, chastised by his dad, who was making $12.50 a week, Willie flashed the bills and gave them to him. Mr. Papaleo was startled and then added, "Willie, can you fight twice a week?"

TONY JANIRO, THE handsome boxing whiz from Youngstown, Ohio, who played such a prominent role in Raging Bull, never completed his education and wasn't the most erudite guy ever. After a brilliant decision win, who entered his dressing room but Harry S. Truman, vice president of the United States at the time under Franklin Delano Roosevelt. After congratulating Tony for his win, he left. Tony asked his manager, "What's he vice-president of, Madison Square Garden"?

THEY DIDN'T COME any tougher, meaner or nastier than Harry Greb, The Pittsburgh Windmill. The middleweight champ even threw a few well-directed punches at any referee who wouldn't let him fight inside.

Weight disparities meant little to the 165-lb. marvel and he fought in three weight divisions, being the only one fighter ever to defeat Gene Tunney.

Greb desperately wanted to fight Jack Dempsey and would wait outside the training camp of the Manassa Mauler day after day. As Dempsey entered and left, Greb shouted at the champ, "Why don't you fight me, you yellow bastard." Harry never got the chance. At age 31, he died on the operating table attempting to fix an eye problem caused by an errant blow in one of his hundreds of fights. He was a great one.

GENE TUNNEY, ONE of the must astute and intellectual champs ever, was also a wizard at handling his finances. The man who loved to read Shakespeare in training camp received one of the biggest paychecks ever for beating Jack Dempsey in the famous "long count" bout in Chicago in 1927. In those pre-tax, non-inflation times, his cut was $990,000.

When Gene picked up his share, he wrote his own personal check for $10,000 and gave it to Tex Ricard, the promoter. "Make one out to me for a million bucks," exclaimed Gene.

Gene Tunney had one more fight, a thrashing of Tom Henney, then married a socialite and retired, a wealthy man. He never made a comeback.

TOUGH TONY PELLONE, the New York City youngster who battled all the leading welterweights of his era, came from a strict upbringing. His father was the Paterfamilias of the stern Italian family and Tony dutifully gave his fight paychecks to his Dad.

After his second main event at Madison Square Garden, a ten round upset win over number-one ranked Billy Graham, his share of the purse was $5,047, which he promptly turned over to the elder Pellone. His Dad gave Tony his allowance, $47.00. Tony, who had a hot date, asked his father for more and Papa gave him three more dollars. "Here, we'll make it an even fifty."

AND THESE GEMS graciously provided by Marty Carson, of Indiana.

Woozel, Boxing and Me

A BOXER ASKED his opponent, "Isn't it a long distance from the dressing room to the ring?" His opponent replied "Yes, but don't worry, you won't have to walk back."

RETURNING TO HIS corner after a busy round, a boxer asked his Second, "Have I done him any damage?" Disgustedly, the Second answered, "No, but keep swinging. The draft might give him a cold."

A BOXING INSTRUCTOR, after giving a pupil his first lesson, "Now, have you any questions to ask?" The dazed beginner replies, "Yes, how much is your correspondence course?"

A BOXING INSTRUCTOR says to his pupil, "That was what they call a half hook" Rubbing his jaw, the pupil says "Well, you can keep the other half."

WHEN KING LEVINSKY met Joe Louis in Chicago's Comiskey Park in the summer of '35, in two minutes and twenty one seconds he was hammered to the deck three times, setting on the bottom rope in a neutral corner the Kingfish asked the referee to stop the fight. "Don't let him hit me again, I'm through," he pleaded. He didn't want to fight the brown bomber. Jack Parr once remarked on his late night show in New York that Levinsky was the first guy he ever saw carried INTO the ring.

RETURNING TO HIS dressing room after a punishing night, a boxer, looking drawn and haggard, for he had taken a terrific beating in the ring, he felt absolutely done in and looked it. When his promoter approached him, he opened his eyes. "Hard times, Jack," he said, as he looked down on his battered charge, "but I've got good news for you." "What's the good news," Jack replied. "I've been lucky enough to arrange a return match for you," answered the promoter.

TIRED OF BEING repeatedly beaten and paid the minimum purse for a bout, a young fighter hit upon a unique idea. He sold advertising space on the bottom of his shoes. For instance, "Eat at Joe's."

A REPORTER CALLED at the residence of a young boxer for an interview. His wife answered the door and when he asked to see the young fighter, she acidly replied, "He is not up yet. Since he became a professional pugilist, he hasn't ever gotten up before the stroke of ten."

THE GREAT JOHN L. SULLIVAN was asked why he had never taken to giving boxing lessons. "Well son, I tried once," he replied. "A husky young man took one lesson from me and went home a little worse for the wear. When he came around for his second lesson he said: 'It was my idea to learn enough about boxing from you to be able to lick a certain young gentleman that I've got it in for. But I've changed my mind. If it's all the same to you Mr. Sullivan, I'll send this young gentleman down here to take the rest of my lessons for me.'"

A YOUNG, UP and coming heavyweight returning wobbly to his corner, promptly dropped down on his stool and asked for water. His second said, "You're doing great, Joe, keep it up." Joe replied, "Keep an eye on that referee, someone's beating the crap out of me."

THE FIRST BLACK heavyweight champion, Jack Johnson, loved to race his vehicles when on the road. When Joe Louis was to meet Max Schmeling in 1938, old Jack was passing through Georgia on his way to the fight and was pulled over by a state policeman for speeding. The charge for a speeding ticket, he was informed, was fifty dollars. Johnson said, upon handing the officer a hundred dollar bill, "Take this hundred, I'll be coming back this way."

ASKED ABOUT HIS YOUTH, when making his comeback, George Foreman said, "You stayed away from me unless you were really curious about trouble."

IT DOESN'T HAPPEN OFTEN, but one time in Reno, Nevada, when two fighters knocked themselves down at the same time, and got up at the same count, it wasn't nine.

WONDERF IF THE ASPCA would take action if they found out, that on a bet, Roberto Duran, once knocked out a horse. Duran was clearly a foe not to horse around with.

ANOTHER INTERESTING AND true story took place on TV, in 1993, when comebacking Bazooka Limon took on Sharmba Mitchell. Limon, whose comeback was short-lived, got so frustrated that he pulled down Mitchell's trunks. It was quite a television debut for Sharma.

SOME ADVICE FROM Joe Svinth of Washington State on how underdogs overcome favorites in boxing matches.
Have a good promoter, e.g. Jack Hurley, Cus D'Amato. Bad examples, Pimp du jour, pick one.

Ring Humor and More

Pick your opponents carefully. As Jake LaMotta once said: "Some you lose, some they tell you to lose. It doesn't have to be the Mob, either. Young Stribling is a case in point.

Wrap yourself in the flag, and avoid flaunting public morality. Joe Louis and Tiger Flowers are examples of this being done well, whereas Jack Johnson is a prime example of it being done poorly.

Learn how to carry a lousy opponent, especially a lousy opponent with a home field advantage.

Keep enough in reserve so that no matter what, you can stand, back up and finish that fight in one. Holmes vs. Shavers is an excellent example of this being done. Leonard vs. Duran is an example of this not being done.

Finally, tip the sportswriters. During Prohibition, Tex Rickard used to give big city sportswriters who said good things about his fighters a case of Scotch. If that's too rich for your blood, then at least give exclusives to your favorite sportswriter, the way Hurley used to do with Emmett Watson of the P-I.

MARLON STARLING WAS asked about a potential fight with Lloyd Honeyghan and he replied, "I'll fight Honeyghan for nothing, if the price is right." (Submitted by Iceman John Scully.)

$5.58, the amount Mike Tyson listed his earnings at in bankruptcy court, as his earnings for November 2003.

THERE ARE A ton of Lou Duva stories out there, to the best of my knowledge, all true. One time, when Lou was managing Andrew 'The Foul Pole' Golota, was asked about the low blows that got Golota disqualified in a fight. Lou responded "Maybe next time I'll have him fight a midget.

One time Lou had an Italian policeman fill in for a fighter who had taken off before the fight. Lou's instructions were simple: "Dance around and don't get hit." The cop danced around until round four, when he, obviously tired, was knocked out. A reporter began asking the fighter some questions. "The guy's Italian and don't speak English," Lou responded, when the fighter couldn't come up with an answer. Alas, the reporter was of Italian descent and started questioning the fighter in Italian. The cop/fighter just shrugged, so Lou again jumped in: "He speaks an obscure, Italian regional dialect."

FROM RICK REENO at Boxingscene.com come these memorable quotes:

"Yesterday I was lying, today I am telling the truth," Bob Arum says to a question asked by a reporter'

After being knocked out - "Mike Tyson dropped me. When I looked up, the count was on five. I said to myself, "Damn, whatever happened to one to four." Buster Mathis Jr. said after his bout with Mike Tyson.'

After Buster Douglas knocked out Tyson in Tokyo, George Foreman said: "He is just like Humpty Dumpty. They are not going to be able to put Tyson back together again."

On Vinnie Pazienza fighting Greg Haugen, "Because this is a title fight, I can have four people in the corner and I will have an extra cut-man. I will also have an extra stool, one for Vinnie to sit on, and the other to throw at him if he doesn't listen to me." Said by Lou Duva.

On his shaven head, "With four sisters about the house, I could never get my hands on a comb." Said by Marvin Hagler.

"Here I predict Sonny Liston's dismemberment, I will hit him so hard, and he will forget where October/November went." Said By Muhammad Ali.

"I'm so fast I could hit you before God gets the news." Said by Muhammad Ali.

"Joe Frazier is so ugly they ought to donate his face to the World Wildlife Fund." Said by Muhammad Ali.

"I'll beat Floyd Patterson so bad, he will need a shoehorn to put his hat on." Said by Muhammad Ali.

Ring Humor and More

"I want to keep fighting because it's the only thing that keeps me out of the hamburger joints. If I don't fight, I'll eat this planet." Said by George Foreman.

"The Internal Revenue Service is the real undefeated heavyweight champion. They show you the left. You never see the right. They will take everything, even your tears." Said by George Foreman'

"Sugar Ray Leonard's retirements lasted about as long as Elizabeth Taylor's marriages." Said by George Foreman'

"Don King doesn't care about black or white. He just cares about green." Said by Larry Holmes.'

"Before Don King started insulting me I was a complete unknown in this country. Now people stop me and ask for my autograph." Said by British promoter Frank Maloney'

On the award of the keys to the city of Scranton, Pennsylvania, to Don King - "Since then we have changed the locks". Said by Mayor James McNutty'

"I fought Sugar Ray Robinson so many times that I'm lucky I didn't get diabetes." Said by Jake Lamotta'

Lennox Lewis was asked as to why he didn't sign with Don King after winning a gold medal. He replied, "How can you trust a guy who never stops talking and you can't understand a word he says."

Buddy McGirt was asked by Gil Clancy on the air who would win the up-coming fight between Maurice Blocker and Glenwood Brown. He replied, "The black guy."

Bob Arum after HIS fighter Iran Barkley beat Darien Van Horn. "If you think Barkley was mad before the fight, wait until he sees how many people are taking part of his purse."

Johnny Carson once asked Sugar Ray Leonard, "When do the wounds from the fight heal"? His reply was, "When the check clears."

"My main objective is to be professional but to kill him." Said by Mike Tyson regarding Lennox Lewis'

After failing an Army intelligence test, "I said that I was the greatest, not the smartest." Said by Muhammad Ali.

"I'm so mean I make medicine sick." Said by Muhammad Ali.

"You need the whole package - boxing, interval training, weights, nutrition, rest, everything. I combine all of them together so I can become like a machine up in that ring." Said by Oscar De La Hoya.

"A champion shows who he is by what he does when he is tested. When a person gets up and says "I can still do it," he is a champion. Said by Evander Holyfield.

"The Glory is the issue to me. Money comes and goes, but a legacy stays forever. I hate to lose." Said by Shane Mosley.

"I want to rip out his heart and feed it to him. I want to kill people. I want to rip their stomachs out and eat their children." Said by Mike Tyson toward Lennox Lewis.

"I felt Holyfield was using his head illegally. I told the referee I wasn't getting any help, so I went back to the streets. I cannot defend it, but it happened." Said by Mike Tyson regarding the ear biting of Evander Holyfield.

"Anyone with a grain of sense would know that if I punched my wife I would rip her head off. It's all lies. I have never laid a finger on her." Said by Tyson regarding allegations he beat his wife'

"In a heavyweight fight, If you don't get up by the count of ten, they stop the fight." Said by Lennox Lewis after his loss to Hasim Rahman.

No chapter would really be complete without a Lou Duva story or quote: When training Andrew "The Foul Pole" Golota: "He's the kind of a kid that gets up at 6 o'clock every morning no matter what time it is".

THERE'S NOTHING LIKE some self deprecating humor, and so I must tell this true story of an event that lead up to the prefight press conference in Sacramento when Ike Ibeabucchi was to fight David Tua in a war.

A FEW DAYS BEFORE the press conference, I was writing an article for Ringsports.com magazine, and had absolutely no idea who Ibeabucci was. I called a friend on the East Coast, who thought I was kidding around when I asked about Ike. Over the phone came a long pause and he went on to tell me that Ibeabucchi had the makings to become the first Japanese Heavyweight champion.

Not knowing that this supposedly ally was pulling my leg, and not having a chance to verify the info that my very knowledgeable friend had provided, I wrote that Ike was indeed from Japan. The looks at the press conference when my magazine was handed out (I was told this by a friend who attended) proved the rule that one should check their sources no matter how good you know your confidant. For the record, Ibeabucchi is from Nigeria.

AND THIS GEM from California timekeeper Mike North. "One time a fighter with his back against the ropes, taking a beating, actually leaned over and asked me to ring the bell."

FRED RYAN OF the Grand Ave Gym in Portland, tells of the time when he was taking down fight posters, and ran out of his car (parked illegally for a moment) with a hammer in his hands, scaring the dickens out of the five people waiting at the bus stop, who saw this seemingly crazed individual coming at them full speed, hammer in hand.

AFTER BEING KNOCKED out in the 13th round by Joe Louis, well ahead on the scorecards, and being told by his corner that all he had to do to win the fight is stay away from Louis, Bill Conn said when asked why he mixed it up with the Brown Bomber: "What's the sense of being Irish, if you can't be stupid?

Woozel, Boxing and Me

PHOTOGRAPHER GREG MARNANE adds this: "My ring nickname was 'Kid Candle' because one blow and I was out."

PROFESSOR LAURENCE MCNAMEE tells of the time in 1991, when Billy Conn and his wife were arguing, and she says "Billy, I heard it three times, but you keep forgetting it. How come I remember and you can't?" To which Billy responded, "I was hit by Joe Louis, you weren't".

ZERRICK WOOLFSON, A boxing fan was kind enough to pass these along:

A truthful anecdote: In my early amateur boxing days in Dublin, Ireland, our trainer was a dour man with beady eyes, a flattened/bent nose, who had been the Irish Bantamweight Champion for six successive years, as well as Golden Gloves or European Champion or both. He was that good, shifty, punched hard with both hands and if he'd turned pro, I'm positive, all things being equal, would have been a World Champ. His name was Frankie Kerr.

One day after sparring with our middleweight, who'd hit him a real thump low on his hip, Frankie stopped sparring and hopped around on one leg. "Dunbar." he yelled, "you should be a light heavyweight." This gratified Dunbar immensely, as he wasn't really that good. "Yes," roared Frankie again. "Light in the head, and heavy on the feet"! The whole gym was in an uproar for about ten minutes, and people still tell the story about, this day, some sixty years later.

FORMER TOUGH AND top Canadian heavyweight George Chuvalo wanted to win the Commonwealth title by fighting and beating Henry Cooper of the U.K. When told of this, Cooper reportedly commented: "I do not want to meet Chuvalo socially, never mind in the ring."

Ring Humor and More

BIG GEORGE FORMAN has long been noted for his sense of humor to go along with his size. George relates this story to Ringsports.com Ireland correspondent Thomas Myler: "I was a 19-year-old-boy who never had a dream come true before. When everyone else was dreaming of a car, I was dreaming of a sandwich."

MIKE TYSON, ON his career after losing to Danny Williams: "I guess I'm just gonna fade into Bolivian."

TYSON AGAIN AFTER being thanked for confronting a suspicious person in his Phoenix neighborhood: "Now I'm the neighborhood watch! I'm Spider-Man"!

HEAVYWEIGHT ANDREW GOLOTA after losing via first round knockout to Lamon Brewster: "I can't believe this happens to me every decade." In 1997, eight years earlier, Golota was knocked out in the first round by Lennox Lewis.

AND FROM WORLD CLASS BOXING JUDGE and friend Glen Hamada:

ABOUT A YEAR and half ago, (2003) Louie Burke of New Mexico was covering a boxing match in Ruidoso, New Mexico for a boxing publication. Louie was once a professional boxer and had a decent ring record. Burke decided at an early age to not continue boxing, however he stayed in the sport by becoming involved with the New Mexico Commission working with the late Jim Boggio.

Louie decided to cover this fight for a boxing publication and not represent the commission.

When he attended the weigh-in, the promoter had some major problems with some of the boxers, including a main event boxer, deciding to pull out. Louie saw that the event was about to fall apart, and the promoter asked Louie if he would be the main event boxer in order to save the show. It had been several years since Louie was in the gym, but he let the promoter entice him to participate. Louie agreed to get into the ring, on one condition, that the event be an exhibition only.

The fight went on and Louie Burke won a unanimous decision against a club fighter that was fighting on a regular basis. Louie is also the brother of Rocky Burke, a New Mexico referee.

IS THERE A RULE about a fighter having sex when in training? Fred Ryan of Portland tells this story about one of his fighters.

I had kept this kid sequestered in his training and lectured him on the evils of pleasures of the flesh in the weeks leading up to his pro debut, and now I was wrapping his hands. Wrapping a kid's hands is a good time to speak with your fighter and to keep him focused, and so I began: "Are you thinking about winning this bout"? "No," he said, "I'm going to win this bout. I was thinking about pussy." He won in a first round KO."

Round IV
More About Woozel

AS I'VE SAID, Sue loved Vegas, it was her kind of City (not mine, although I do have an awful lot of great friends there, it's just too damn hot and dusty for my taste).

I REMEMBER WHEN we we're staying at the timeshare and the noisy crickets were everywhere, including all over our room, and were even glad to visit with us by the outdoor hot tub. It was far from being ready made for romance. I went up to the gal at the front desk telling her, "I don't mind the crickets so much, but it would have been much better if you would have brought along Buddy Holly also." I got another strange look.

SUE USED TO love to lie around the pool and the hot tub, taking in the sun, and although she knew sun bathing wasn't my thing, she would always say, "Don't be a damn pussy. Besides who's going to put the lotion on my back and do (massage) my feet"? Most of the time, I willingly obliged her. But I always made sure I was located under an umbrella or whatever shade there was available. Being light skinned I burn easily. Besides I am not a sun worshiper. I'll leave that to others.

I RECALL THERE was the time that Wuz hung her wet clothes on the ceiling fan in the timeshare studio to dry, and forgot all about them, turned the fan on and her damp/wet clothes landed everywhere with two even flying out the open patio screen door and landing two flights down. Since she wasn't wearing anything, I had to make the short trek downstairs to retrieve them, and of course explain to those who had the inquiring minds that the clothes flying over the balcony didn't mean that we were having a wild sex party, although that would have been fun. Who knows what they thought or believed?

IN RENO THERE came a time that Sue and I had a business party to go to in the evening, and she came over that afternoon to spend some time. After a brief encounter I found she had left her white silk panties in my apartment. Wuz was just getting off her period so she had the panties with her but she didn't need them.

With the good intentions of wanting to return the item, I put them in my back pocket and was going to hand them to her in a private moment. Sadly, I had forgotten completely about them while the wine was flowing (so to speak). Suddenly I had to sneeze and when I reached into my back pocket for a handkerchief, I instead pulled out her panties, which I ungracefully sneezed into.

Sue's face turned about ten shades of red, while I held the panties up in surprise. Everyone at the party was laughing, and Wuz quickly joined in the laughter as well, commenting on the shape of my new silk handkerchief.

SUE HAD ONCE told me a story which if it were anyone else, I'd never have believed. She was living with her husband (at the time), Don, at their home in Yerington, and he took her and Dorian camping. Wuz found a package of some laxative chewing gum. As usual, not reading the label, so not knowing the effect, Sue chewed and swallowed the entire package. Need I say more?

SUE ALWAYS LIKED to live on the edge. While she never really was hurting for money, she liked to go to thrift stores and look for bargains. She usually dragged me with her, not that I particularly liked thrift stores, but I did enjoy her company, and I was, on rare occasion, able to purchase some pretty decent clothes, cheap. She was also in the habit of squeezing every drop out of her makeup. It made no sense, but that was my Wuzzel.

WUZ ALSO ENJOYED drinking and gambling, usually but not exclusively with me, with slots and Keno being her favorite games. There were many times when she was depressed and didn't want to go home, just drink and gamble till all the money was gone. And on occasion this somewhat annoying habit would make me late for any appointments. I couldn't let her drive herself home in that condition, so I had to wait until she was finished. I hate to say it, but there were times I couldn't wait for her to lose her money, just to come close to keeping a scheduled appointment.

SUE WOULD GET angry at me on some or our trips because when we couldn't find our destinations easily, I asked her to look at the map and give me the directions. Unfortunately she didn't know how to read a road map. Heck, she didn't know East from West. Sue also couldn't find her way out of a paper bag and would gladly admit that to anyone. Wuz had no sense of direction at all, and freely admitted it. But she sure was good at making insulting statements to me like "Any man I've ever been with would be able to find the place." Of course most of the men she was with abused her, thus could not be described as men, and I would never have stooped to that level.

Her any man could do better than Rusty routine took a funny turn when we spent a night at the Silver Club late in 1986. The toilet was running, and when jiggling the handle did no good, I lifted the tank top to be greeted with a spray of water all over my face. "God, you are so damn helpless," she exclaimed, "Any other man I know could fix this toilet, and Even *I* can fix it". So, to prove her point she went into the bathroom, and upon lifting the tank top she too was greeted with a spray of water all over her pretty face. That was my laugh for the day and Wuz, muttering under her breath, dried herself off and called the front desk for maintenance.

WE WERE IN Stockton, California, looking for her son Dorian, who was having his girlfriend at the time, make a bar-b-que for us at one of his "friends" houses. This gal had a very odd sounding name or nickname. The name escapes me now, but I can clearly remember the strange looks Wuz got when searching for her house. We knew that we were in Dorian's girlfriend's neighborhood and she asked the local Hispanics who lived there if they knew 'where Puta lived'. Of course her name sounded like, but certainly was not, Puta. For those of you who don't speak the language, Puta means bitch in Spanish. I remained in the car, sliding down in the seat, laughing, with tears rolling down my cheeks.

THEN THERE WAS a time I went with Sue shopping at a local supermarket, when some weird chick confronted her and asks her if she could "pick up her keys with her pussy"? Of course that angered Sue, and she went after her, leaving me to once again jump between her and someone much taller and possibly younger, and since Sue was on chemo, probably much stronger.

However, fortunately nothing came of it. But for some strange reason these were the people that Wuz seemed to attract.

LIKE MOST MEN, I've had the zipper on my fly rip at some embarrassing places. Once when I was covering the Davis Cup at Caesars Palace in Las Vegas, and having no backup, I had to figure a way to get to a nearby department store and solve the problem, which, with (some safety pins) and the help of my wife Lois, I did.

ONE LATE AFTERNOON in the fall I was sitting with Sue at the Silver Club, along with a lot of folks, watching Sunday football. Suddenly I felt a draft, looked down to find that my zipper had ripped at some point earlier. I walked to the bathroom to try to fix it and found that there was nothing I could do. After about five minutes, I got Sue's attention and called her over to where I was wall hugging at the side of the men's room.

Her first reaction to my situation was her famed "let me see." I told her to forget that for now, just find me some safety pins. She took off and was gone for 45 minutes. Returning she apologized for taking so long, and produced only one safety pin that was blue at the ends and was a couple of inches in length. Something you'd probably find at a circus.

Having little choice, I used the pin. I then told Sue to walk alongside me, down the stairs and to the parking garage where I'd drive home and change my pants. I asked her not to look down or laugh, which needless to say was her cue to do just the opposite. She waited till we were halfway across the room when she looked at my fly, and burst out laughing, causing me to want to strangle her and depart even quicker.

For a few hours after we got to my apartment, Sue swore up and down that neither the pin nor the laughter at my expense was intentional, but not long after that she told me that she "couldn't pass up such a great opportunity."

HAVING GLAUCOMA AND other eye problems, I make it a point never to drive at night, but sometimes you just have to make an exception.

On one such occasion, I got a phone call from Sue on a very snowy New Years Eve. She was in jail, and obviously had more than a few drinks before being arrested. But it wasn't the alcohol that had gotten Sue locked up.

Sue had a fight (not unusual) with Dorian, and *she* called the police to get him out of her apartment. When the gendarmes arrived, they asked her if they could search her house. Of course she gave permission. During that search they discovered some drugs hidden in her sofa, which of course Sue didn't know anything about or she certainly wouldn't have allowed the search.

The police handcuffed both her and her son and took them to the jail. Snow or not, Sue refused to even put on her shoes when arrested, leaving her apartment barefoot.

So it was almost midnight and Wuz calls my house and tells me to get her out of this place, there are a bunch of druggies and alcoholics there (what would she have expected, especially on New Years Eve). Sue continued to call and my wife Lois had to calm her down until I made it to the jail.

I got dressed jumped into the car and took the half-hour or so drive from my house to the jail. I stopped by the bail bondsman and put up our house as a bond. One thing about Sue, she would never steal from me or anyone else. Whatever shortcomings she may have had, dishonesty was not one of them.

So I picked her up at the jail and she walked to the car, still without shoes on. I took her home and she made it up the stairs to her house without any trouble. Of course she showed up in court when she had to. She was about as far from a flight risk as a dodo bird.

SUE'S MOM, AMELIA, was a classy lady who was blessed with a long and happy life. She knew how I felt about Sue, and seemed to approve of us being together as man and wife (this was before I met Lois). But it certainly wasn't Sue's idea. Sue just wanted to be friends and share good times together. She too believed we were soul mates, but didn't want to marry me. Her reason at that juncture was that *'we were too much alike'*, and *'opposites attract'*.

Shortly before she passed away she told me that I was her "*hero,*" whatever that meant.

Her mom was never very good at telling jokes. Once, before a Christmas party at her house, Sue had earlier prompted her mom with a simple joke. "Did you hear the joke about the cookie?" and when no one would answer, her mom was supposed to say, "Well, it was crumby, anyway." The party was in full swing when Sue told everyone that her mom had a great joke to tell. Amelia promptly asked: "Did you hear the joke about the cookie?" and when no one responded, she said "Well, it was lousy anyway"

THE LAST YEAR or two of her life, though, Sue would reduce her drinking consider-ably, and her gambling substantially. One of the reasons, I believe, was that I wouldn't meet her in any casinos that had low ceilings, as the smoke would be bad for her. As for the drinking, she slowed down on her own. Because of the chemo even alcohol tasted bad to her most of the time.

But Wuz did have a girlfriend who had a bad gambling habit, and knew that Sue had cancer. Yet Sue stayed up all night with her gambling on more then one occasion. I do believe that was one of the things that shortened her life, as that, along with all the stress, weakened her immune system.***

ON A PERSONAL NOTE, Wuz was watching our house (which she always would do when Lois and I left for vacation) while we took off on a cruise to the Mexican Riviera.

On 'the boat's dress up' night, Lois designed some clothes that made me look like a Priest and herself like a Nun.

More About Woozel

We tried on the outfits, and instead of taking the time to change, we wore them when we docked in Mexico and Lois went down the gangplank to get the USA Today, while I waited for her return at the top of the plank.

At this point a young gal who had been drinking at a local bar came staggering up the gangplank, saw me in my Priests garb, and quickly crossed herself, asking my forgiveness for her sin.

I never get taken aback for long, so I told her to say seven 'hail Mary's' and go to her room, which to my surprise, she quickly did, thanked me and headed for her cabin.

That evening at the dinner, the Mexican band asked 'Father Rusty' what song I would like to hear. Needless to say I chose 'Ave Maria', and they were more than happy to comply.***

INDIANA JUDGE GARY Merritt tells the story of a fight that happened in Davenport, Iowa, on October 18, 1995. Their fight was a fight between Lonnie Horn and Craig Houk. Houk was balding and wearing a hairpiece that he had glued on earlier in the week.

It was a hot, humid evening and early in the fight Horn landed a jab and Houk's hair became unglued and lifted up and would continue to do so on every punch Horn landed. Later in the fight Craig was knocked down, and his hairpiece slides almost to the canvas. Craig reached back and put the wig back in place. The headline in the local paper the next day said it was "a hair raising fight." The tape of the fight made America's Funniest Sports Videos.

Promoter Fred Berns takes the story a step further. "Before the fight, Craig went down to Florida to spar with Christy Martin. She was beating the crap out of him and knocking his headgear around, which loosened up the glue on his wig a little bit. He didn't have time to go for his hair treatment. He went straight to Davenport for the fight. Horn keeps hitting him in the wig. Craig goes down, hits his head against the bottom rope, and the rug flipped over.

Dick Clark did a sports blooper video on the hair rising piece, and they used the Houk knockdown as the commercial for it. Houk was so embarrassed, he moved away. Then he got a high priced law firm to sue Dick Clark. At the preliminary hearing the law firm states that the wrong guy is suing as the rights to the video belong to the promoter, Fred Berns, and he should be suing Dick Clark. However they did stop using the film clip.***

BERNS CONTINUES: "ONE of the most terrifying times I ever had was when I had the 'Fighting Senator' Ken Snyder on one of my cards. When I get into the arena, there was no ring. The guy who was supposed to set it up wouldn't answer the phone.

"The crowd was starting to pile into the arena. The guy who Fred hired to set up the ring was with the Golden Gloves, and when we got to the house he said that he didn't feel like going to the arena. After explaining to the guy that it wasn't his ring, I had one of my guys rent a truck. It took us three hours to set up the ring. The fight card was supposed to start at 7 PM and it started after 10:00."

ANOTHER STORY OUT of the Midwest was told by fight judge Nick Price. "We were doing a fight in Indianapolis. One of the fighters sitting close to ringside was Nate Lenore, who wasn't scheduled to fight that evening. He was asked if he'd like to fight for a trophy. Nate said "Why not"? He was already wearing his tennis shoes. He stripped, we put the gloves on him and he went to ring-center to receive instructions. He suddenly got this panicked look on his face. He turned around, looked several different ways, turned around and ran back to the corner. I asked him what was going on. And he said he had to get his pistol out of his pocket. He's the only fighter I know of who's ever gotten into the ring carrying a handgun. The guy won the fight, but Price had to sit on his pistol all evening.***

I REMEMBER SITTING at ringside for a local (Reno) club fight when I heard a couple of boxers sitting behind me talking. "Hey, man. Glad to see your out (of jail) and back on the right track." "Yeah, it's great to be free and I'm going to the top now and nothing's gonna stop me. Nothing! I'm never going to do anything wrong again….unless I have to." I don't know if he had to, but he certainly never became a champion in the ring.

I CAN RECALL THE night that a boxer came into the ring at a fight at Lake Tahoe with *very* tight trunks, and there was a bad moon rising all night, as the trunks ripped down the entire back seam early in the contest, but the fight continued and the fighter made a perfect ass out of himself..

I REMEMBER ANOTHER night at the Lake when a fighter named Paddy Wilson, who I had never seen sober, in or out of the ring was fighting in a prelim. He was even lit up the few times I saw him training. On this evening, in round one, Paddy had a haymaker thrown at him that missed by a mile and yet Wilson went to the canvas. Referee Mills Lane, who was never one to take any nonsense, bent over Wilson and told him, "If you expect to get paid this night, you'd better get up and fight." It was a good thing that Mills didn't light a match. Wilson got up, quickly, took a couple of serious punches and went down and out, legitimately.

BOXING HAS ATTRACTED a lot of famous people, some as boxers, most as fans. The late comedian Bob Hope boxed in his native England and had this to say about his brief and infamous pugilistic career. "I ruined my hands in the ring. The referee kept stepping on them."

Woozel, Boxing and Me

WHILE I AM considered mainly a boxing writer (others who don't like me probably consider me something much worse) one of my fortes is doing interviews. It gives you an insight into what makes the person tick and helps create a certain bond with that individual.

I've had the pleasure of interviewing the late, great publicist Irving Rudd, who was a class act, in capital letters. I've had the fun of interviewing Randall "Tex" Cobb, and Bert Sugar, who both happen to be two of the brightest and nicest guys you ever want to meet, in or out of the boxing business, not to mention a couple of the funniest and most spontaneous people I've ever been fortunate enough to meet. Needless to say I also picked the brilliant mind of my late, good friend and legendary trainer Eddie Futch, on more than one occasion.

PHIL MORTON, MY partner at the time with Ring Arts Magazine, went with me to Cobb's hotel room at Bally's, Reno, to do the interview. Tex was expecting us, but we didn't expect to have him answer the door stark naked. It was good that Wuz wasn't with us, although knowing her, she probably would have enjoyed it. Tex closed the door, looked at the business card and remarked, "Ring Arts, you guys are a household name, I bet everyone in your household knows who you are."

When asked why Cobb, a college graduate from Texas would be fighting for a living, he simply replied: "Hell darlin' it beats laying concrete all to hell".

Tex was in Reno to fight Eddie Gregg on the undercard of Larry Holmes/Carl 'The Truth' Williams title go. He was knocked down during the bout and lost the decision. At the press conference after the fight, one of the reporters asked him how it felt being knocked to the mat for the first time in his career. Tex took a swig of his beer, and said: "Hell darlin', I go down a lot. Just don't tell my wife!" There are plenty of more Tex Cobb stories to go around, but in the interest of space, and truth (since I was there) I'll just stick to these two that I witnessed in person.

On that same night, a guy working Gregg's corner was heard to say: "Go out there and get him. Do you want to go back to selling pencils on the street corner"?

Tex Cobb has always boasted that his claim to fame was getting newsman Howard Cosell out of pro boxing, after taking a tremendous beating at the hands of Larry Holmes in 1982. Before this, and before I had the non-pleasure to meet him in person, I thought Cosell was an outstanding announcer and was good for the sport. Shows how little I knew back then.

I had the dubious honor of introducing myself to Cosell at an amateur pre-Olympic event at Lawlor Events Center in Reno. I believe it was the USA vs. Cuba. I made my way to ringside before the fight to shake his hand and show him our publication. His attitude was lousy at best. "I don't care who you are or who you write for" he said, his hands trembling from Parkinson's. "All boxers are whores and everyone like you, who make a living off them are nothing but fucking pimps"!

I was taken aback. If Cosell wasn't so old and rickety he would have been the first astronaut launched without the benefit of a spaceship. I turned and walked away, his once-bright image ruined forever in my eyes.***

REFEREE STEVE SMOGER worked a Mickey Rourke fight in Germany. Rourke had called him on the phone and wanted him as the referee. He said Rourke did everything right warming up. Rourke was hitting the pads in the dressing room, shadow boxing and working out. Before Rourke got his gloves on Smoger came back and Rourke was smoking a cigarette, which was highly unusual. Rourke started to laugh because he got caught. Cigarette or not, he ended up winning the four-round fight.***

I HAVE BEEN FORTUNATE enough to spend a few good hours with perhaps the busiest and certainly the funniest, Midwest promoter Fred Berns, an ex-Chicago-cop, now living and promoting in Indianapolis. Fred is not only funny, but very outspoken about any and all issues both in and out of boxing. Fred's stories can keep you laughing for days on end. If you ask him about Bruce "Mouse" Strauss, who he worked with at times, he may just keep the conversation going forever.

I'VE HAD THE PLEASURE of getting to know Lou Duva, a man I both like and respect. Lou's one of those kind of guys that it takes a while to get to know, but once you do, he's always your friend.

There are also a lot of great Lou Duva stories around. Once, when he was working the corner for a young Evander Holyfield, The "Real Deal" came back to his corner after a bad round, and Lou threw some cold water in his face and said: "Do you know what the hell you're doing out there"? When Holyfield answered yes, Lou said, "Good, now don't do it again"!

Another favorite Duva story was when he was training John –John Molina in Virginia Beach, Virginia. Molina wanted to train all the time, so to keep him busy, after a tough workout, Lou told him to run to the first red light and come back. An hour-and-a-half later an exhausted Molina returned. When Lou asked where he had been for so long, John simply said "All the lights were green."

ANOTHER VERY BRIGHT and funny gentleman is Hall of Fame boxing writer and historian Bert Sugar, who knows boxing as well as anyone around and whom I consider a friend. Bert has some great stories as well, and is a big plus for our profession. I've known Bert for some time and consider a major resource foe needed boxing or sports information.

Bert told me that he wears his famous hat because in the old days, they used hot lead (rivets) to set the type, and they would sometimes burn through the wooden floor and land on the head of anyone passing by--thus the hat.

Bert also told me that when he was growing up, his first love was baseball and that he wanted to be a ballet dancer and went to ballet school with Shirley MacLaine. Don't know if he was pulling my leg on the latter. There are few, if any, around today more knowledgeable about boxing than Bert.***

ONE OF THE MORE enjoyable interviews I did was in Portland, Oregon, with Hall of Famer and ex world champion, Carmen Basilio, who along with his wife Josie, still do a lot for the image of our sport. Guys like Carmen can only be seen one way, *CLASS PERSONIFIED*. And there are many, many guys out there, like Carmen, who have given and continue to give to the sport they love.

I HAVE MET MUHAMMAD ALI a few times. Sadly, the Ali of today, who has Parkinson's Syndrome, is not the way I prefer to remember him. He'll always be "the Greatest" and the Ali who could box rings around some of the greatest heavyweights of all time. That is how I'll always remember him.

The last time I met Ali was at the Mirage in Vegas, when Jose Sulaiman, President of the WBC, called me over to his table, where Ali was dining, and asked if I would like to join them. I wanted to and probably should have, but I was running very late for a meeting. But I did notice that Ali had food falling out of the side of his mouth. It was indeed sad to see how the mighty had fallen. But being a fighter, Ali would not let Parkinson's get in the way of him assisting others in need.

I TRIED TO give back to the self proclaimed 'greatest' when I flew to Oakland at my own expense to host a benefit for Ali at Ricky's Sports Bar in the home of 'Raider Nation'. We had two exceptional impersonators on hand, one, Ernie Orozco doing a great impression of Howard Cosell, the other the voice of

Ali, John Ramsey, who does a great job of impersonating the great one.

I'm not one to prepare with anything in writing, always feeling more comfortable in winging it. But I always try to be prepared with a comeback line if my opening falls flat. This time, it was with a simple line, "You think it's easy introducing Howard Cosell, a dead man?"

TO BE HONEST I consider just about everyone I've been fortunate enough to meet in the boxing community, a friend. We're in one of the toughest businesses around and in a sport that probably gets much less respect than any of the others, yet, to a man, (or woman), boxing folks are some of the finest people on this earth.

The list of friends goes on and on, and no matter how hard I try, I know that I'll forget a lot of people if I continue in this vein. To those folks I omitted, I sincerely apologize. Suffice it to say, I love boxing and the many wonderful people in it. The "sweet science" has been very good to me and I hope I have in some small part, been able to return the compliment.

However, I would be remiss not to mention two of my best friends in the business, the late, great trainer Eddie Futch and his gorgeous wife Eva. Eddie knew the game inside and out, and by the time they wed, Eva had picked up much of the knowledge that Eddie had.

Eddie was a dear friend, more like a brother, and I consider Eva, who I've known a long time, a very dear, wonderful person as well. Here was a relationship that could only have been made in Heaven.***

AS FOR MY OLD friend, the late Jack Welsh, he was a well-known sports writer (not just boxing) for many different publications and websites, including our own Ringsports.com.

I had known Jack probably longer then I knew Wuz, and in many ways he was every bit as goofy as she was. But in

More About Woozel

fairness, you have to be somewhat goofy to be in the boxing business.

Jack's favorite dining spot was an Olive Garden in Vegas, and we had eaten there many times. One day we're sitting at the table when the waitress came over to take our order. Jack looks at the menu and then up at her and says, "Whatever happened to the fricasseed owl you had on the menu? It was delicious."

The waitress was new and had absolutely no idea Jack was just pulling her leg. And shortly the chef came out to see who had made the order and giving the waitress a hard time. Jack said, "All I wanted was boiled, de-feathered fricasseed owl filet. I'm sure that I had it here last time."

The chef obviously knew Jack, and just shook his head and asked that he please stop driving his hired help crazy.

When Jack was working for a Philadelphia paper, before moving to Vegas, he was in Sin City to cover a fight. Jack was a heavy drinker at the time and before the bout, sat down at a fight at the Hilton for a few belts. On the seat next to him, he put down a big stuffed dog. He ordered drinks for both himself and his " best friend." When suddenly he turned to the stuffed dog and said: "I've been buying drinks all day and you haven't even offered." And with that he got up and walked away, leaving the bartender with untouched shots by the stuffed dog as well as the tab, which eventually was covered by Jack's friends.

MIKE TYSON HAS long been known for some goofy stunts and comments, as well as his boxing abilities. When he was invited to the San Remo Song Festival in Italy, he said: "I have no idea why they invited me. Maybe it's because I'm a music lover"

Jeffrey Dahmer would get more chances than me," said by Mike Tyson.

Woozel, Boxing and Me

THE NEXT FEW stories were supplied to me by Dr. Robert Quam, D.C., a long-time boxing fan, musician and friend.

Tommy Loughran was having a very rough fight and was losing badly when the referee asked him if he was okay. Loughran turned to the ref and said "I'm fine, and you?"

Max Baer was fighting Joe Louis, who is beating the hell out of him. Jack Dempsey says to Baer, "C'mon Max, he's not hurting you." Baer turns to Dempsey and says: "Then you'd better check the referee, because someone is kicking the shit out of me".

Max Baer on Jimmy Braddock: "Braddock's a nice guy, a family man, wife and kids, I don't have any kids. At least none that I know about."

Baer used to try to get cauliflower ears by banging his head against sewer pipes. One time when he was hurting for money, he started selling percentages of himself and eventually wound up selling 115% of himself.

When Joe Louis was a PFC in the US Army, a sergeant got out of his truck, reamed Louis verbally, and than drove off. Someone asked Joe why he didn't knock the sergeant's block off and Louis said something to this effect: "If someone insulted Caruso's singing, would he sing him an aria"?

One time a world champion asked Joe Louis to stand guard at his hotel room door to watch out for his wife, while he was getting some side action. The champ's wife came by in a huff, passes Louis and catches her husband in the act. Afterward, the fighter comes out of the room and asks, "Joe, why didn't you warn me"? Joe responded, "I was afraid to say anything." The fighter just shook his head and replied: "The heavyweight champion of the world and you're afraid to say anything"!

Former heavyweight champion Jack Johnson when fighting Tommy Burns, lifts up one arm towards the sky, and then the other, as if to say "Hit here, Tommy."

Jack Johnson. the first black heavyweight champion, when fighting Frank Moran, said to him in the ring, trying to bait him, "C'mon Frankie, hit that nigger," and continued to repeat it.

More About Woozel

Muhammad Ali and Joe Frazier were on a TV show promoting their upcoming fight. Ali is doing his "I am the greatest" routine. Then turns to Frazier and says, "Let me tell you something, boy." Joe starts to jump out of his chair, when Ali corrects himself and quickly says, "Roy. I said Roy".

Pittsburgh tough guy Fritzie Zivic went to see his doctor after one of his fights to get his skull x-rayed. After the first set is looked at, the doctor says he wants a second set. Again, the doc seems confused by what he sees and says that he's going to take the next set himself. At this point Fritzie is thinking they may have found something bad. Not the case. The doc comes out and says, "Yours is the thickest skull I've seen in all my years of practicing medicine. It is $3\frac{1}{2}$ times as thick as any skull that I have ever x-rayed".

Round V

It's not all that great

WHILE ALMOST ALL MY memories of boxing have been positive ones, there have been some incidents that occurred that should never have happened.

A PROBLEM OCCURRED, and I'll accept full responsibility (and blame) for this, I always deal with everyone, including my advertisers the old fashioned way, via word of mouth or a handshake. I only used contracts when the advertiser himself would insist upon it. A signature, in my eyes, is only as good as the person signing it.

Because of this sometimes, but rarely misguided trust, I have been screwed out of some much needed revenue on a couple of occasions, but my attitude has always been, if they need the cash more than I do, just forget about it, and we'll both get our just rewards in the end. And in truth these incidents have been so few and far between, it's hardly worth the time to write about them, but I will, without naming names.

One of our debtors was a California Indian Casino, who continually changed marketing folks faster and it seemed like

It's not all that great

far more often than babies have their diapers changed, and the new folks there didn't know of the agreement we had with the original marketing people (or claimed not to know) and never canceled the on-going ad we were running for them. That was to cost us about $1200 out of the pocket of Ring Sports, and it didn't help when the possible choices of bankruptcy or reorganization was forced upon us. That's what happens often when you begin a brand new business on a worn shoestring, and some people are either late or refuse to pay their bills. In this case the right hand had no idea what the left hand had done.

I suppose that I should have learned my lesson, and used the contracts I had readily available, but being a people person, I refused to lower myself to others standards, that would have made sense but would also have shown a distrust in our fellow humans and boxing folk. I believe that's one of the problems with today's society. Although most people are honest, a few spoil it for the rest. Life is much like boxing in that regard.

AND IN RECENT YEARS, I've forgotten about a few ads also, it just happens with getting older and having to live in a bit more pain than one would like.

I had/have been often asked why my some of my many friends didn't help out with the advertising or investments. First of all, I doubt any of them knew the true severity of the financial trouble the magazine was in at the time, and secondly, the few times I asked for advertising help, many would pass the buck to others. I know many of my friends don't necessarily make the final decisions, but they certainly could have told the people who handled it, that they wanted to advertise with Ring Sports, and my guess is that should have been more than sufficient. But they didn't, and it was their decision, and I respect that.

Another reason why some of my close friends wouldn't advertise is because they were involved in boxing first hand, and it could have constituted a conflict of interest for them to do so. Then again, some of my friends who owned businesses outside of boxing quickly stepped up to the plate to help, and I am eternally grateful.

Another problem was that the hotels and casinos just don't understand that to compete with the other kids on the block, now including the Indian casinos which have proliferated and taken revenue out of Nevada, you must advertise in a publication that reaches their base. In Nevada, that would be our publication, yet, ads (boxing or other) were sparse, unless there was a boxing event going on at their venue.

For whatever reasons, these marketing folks didn't understand that a lot of folks outside of Northern Nevada, who come and visit, receive our publication, need a place to eat, sleep and gamble, etc. and want to know what shows to see when visiting. I just could never communicate this to the people in casino marketing that would make the decisions.

On the plus side, many of the great folks, who are my friends in boxing, rallied behind me and kept the publication from going belly-up. Friends like Lee Samuels, Kerry Daigle, Fred Ryan, Shelley Williams, Eva Futch, Denis Nolan, Johnny Wilds, Harrin Platzner, etc. went the extra mile for us, and I will never forget their kindness. They can be on my time till Hell freezes over.

IN 1999, RINGSPORTS HOSTED the 10th anniversary party for the magazine at the Silver Club in Sparks, Nevada. My late friend, great trainer and human being, Eddie Futch and his beautiful, sweet wife, Eva, flew in from Southern California to attend. Eddie was in his mid 80's and not in the best of health, but he had promised me that he was going to be with me for this event, and he was, although he was only able to stay for the Saturday afternoon auction, where he was kind enough to donate a few items, and sign some autographs for those in attendance, before returning home. Eddie came to the event out of his sick bed to be with me and my boxing family, on this very special occasion. That was the kind of guy he was, and his beautiful spouse Eva has always been very much the same.

It's not all that great

And needless to mention, Eddie Futch, in my very humble opinion, was the best boxing trainer who ever lived.

At the big party on Saturday night, I had a friend from Northern California, James Brewster Thompson, better known as "The Ropemaster," who was kind enough to drive to Sparks to entertain. All he asked for was to have his expenses paid, which we gladly did. James would jump rope with 3-5 people hanging on to him at once.

At one point, during the show, he asked my East Coast Editor and friend Jack Hirsch to get on top of his shoulders, wherein Jack politely refused. Since I've always been one to lead by example, I took up the challenge, bad back and knees notwithstanding, and came out of the experience none the worst for wear. The event cost me/the mag a few bucks as a college boxing event in Vegas took away many friends who were going to attend.

I ARRIVED EARLY to a boxing event at Caesars Palace, when I saw Sugar Ray Leonard on stage, preparing for the evenings broadcasting duties. I went up on stage to exchange pleasantries, and asked him for two autographs, one for my wife, Lois and the other for my best friend Sue.

"Wife and girlfriend? Rusty, how did you manage that?" Ray inquired. I responded, "Ray, I may be the only guy in the boxing profession with faster feet than you." He busted up laughing.

ON ANOTHER OCCASION I had just finished a radio gig at the Spice House, a gentleman's club in Reno, and was sitting down to eat dinner, awaiting my ride home. A young gal who obviously was employed there came over to me and asked me if I wanted a dance. Totally oblivious to what she meant, I told her the truth, that I had two left feet. The gal shook her head and walked away, muttering to herself. When I told one of the guys that I was doing the show with about the apparent, "Odd request," he just shook his head. "Rusty, hello, she was talking about a lap dance."

STAYING WITH THE lighter side, there were still a few goofy memories that only Sue could give me during that point in time. For instance, the day that Lois and I got married, Wuz went to the local jail to visit her son before intending to drive back to attend our wedding. Since she was running late (she was almost always late, and Wuz owned more watches then anyone I knew) she asked a stranger in a suit and tie, at the jail, who she thought was (and may well have been) a lawyer, to please lock up her purse for her.

Of course after her brief visit with Dorian was finished and she was about to leave the premises to attend our wedding, the guy and her purse had long since gone, as were her drivers license, money, credit cards, etc. Sue never did show up at our nuptials. Since I knew this was something only Wuz would do, I wasn't upset or surprised.

I recall the time that Sue and I stayed at the Sacramento Hilton for a few days, on the 10th floor and Sue refused to take the elevator, always choosing to be healthy and run the flights of steps, and usually beating me and the elevator. She was younger and seemingly always healthy as a horse back then.

But like so many other folks, Sue always liked to steal good hotel towels, although she used them to wash her car, which seemed to be one of her favorite pastime in life. In short, the bags coming home from any of our trips were always heavier then they when we left Reno.

We were checking out of the Sacramento Hilton and I asked the bellman if he liked boxing. He said yes, and I asked him to come out to the car and I would give him a free copy of my magazine which was in the trunk. He was in his hotel uniform. It was an opportunity not to be passed up.

Sue was packing the car trunk at the time and had the towels and some other cheap goodies that she had made off with on the roof of her auto for packing. I called out to her as we slowly began to walk over. She turned around, quickly. "Sue! Hotel security here! He wants to talk to you and check your luggage," I said. Needless to say she panicked and everything went flying from the top of her car. It was really funny and it was one of the few times I was able to get even for all the gags she pulled on me.

SUE LOVED DOGS, and when her mom's white cocker spaniel, Punch, passed away from cancer, we got the bad news call from her sister. We were in Vegas for a fight, and Sue started crying a lot when she heard the news. We had no idea that Punch was ill, let alone had cancer, when we left for Vegas a week earlier.

Wuz was bound and determined to replace the dog as a live-in companion for her mom. Her mom, Amelia, was against it, until Sue told her she'd just bring her home a little dog to keep her company. Sue went to the pound a few times but finally returned home with a small, good looking pit bull.

When her mom opened the screen door for her and took one look at Jinx, she said, "That's not a cocker spaniel. What the hell is that?" It took awhile for Sue to get her mom to re-open the door and much longer to get her to accept the dog, which turned out to be a very smart, good and faithful companion, except when it saw dogs it didn't like, or any cats and/or birds. It also had a few health problems. Other then that, no major reasons not to keep Jinx.

I CLEARLY REMEMBER a day that Wuz was supposed to come over and watch our house while we played bridge at a friend's home. She was nearing the end of her life at the time, and like a jerk, I forgot to lock the house key in the garage for her.

Sue had brought her golden colored pit bull, Jinx, with her. The color was like Woosie, my Shar Pei/Pit Bull cross. Of course my dog was very fat and very gentle. Jinx jumped over the fence and took off after a young lady walking a Rotweiller. Other than scaring the shit out of the poor lady (and the other dog), Sue was finally able to catch Jinx, get her back into the car and drive home. She left me the following note: "Rusty: You forgot to leave the garage door open for me. You are an ass, like in hole." That was Sue, like me she would rarely get seriously angry. Still, she didn't need the aggravation, which certainly didn't help fight off her cancer.

Imagine my surprise in returning home that evening and finding along with Sue's note, a note from the Animal Control telling me that my dog "Woosie" had jumped the fence and attacked the Rottweiler. I knew Rosie couldn't jump the fence (too fat) and was very gentle. Sue called me later to explain that it was her dog, Jinx that had jumped the fence. The really strange thing was the guy from Animal Control had to know that my dog was gentle and couldn't jump the fence because he walked into our yard and put the note on my front door.

I RECALL A TIME at the Dunes in Las Vegas, when I was with Sue in the swimming pool. Sue splashed me with water and took off, and I took off after her. Half way across the pool, my back totally locked on me, and I didn't remember to float. I panicked instead. this is something I almost never do.

I was going down for the third time when Sue got to me and held me up, while two guys at poolside jumped in and got me on terra firma. They wanted to call an ambulance, as I had no movement in my back at all, but after about five minutes the feeling started to return, and shortly thereafter, I regained my land legs.

Wuz saved my life that day. Even though I know what to do if it were to happen again, I now avoid swimming pools totally, one of the few mental blocks I have.

THERE WAS A TIME when Wuz and I were on the 23rd floor at an L.A. hotel attending the World Boxing Hall of Fame induc-

It's not all that great

tions. A strong, rolling earthquake hit at about 3 a.m. It woke me and just about everyone asleep at the hotel, but Sue had a few too many drinks and was sound asleep. The instructions were to make your way down the stairs, but realistically we were just too high up. The small table being near the window, and having no way to get under the bed, I figured there was no reason for me to wake Wuz up unless I heard buildings going down, at which time I would kiss her goodbye and thank her for all the great years of fun she had given me.

Needless to say I heard a loud bang outside, and logically figured that our time on earth was up, so I gently woke up Sue as I intended to. She got out of bed, ran to the window and said "You fucking idiot! That was a car crash you heard. We had an earthquake and you didn't even bother to wake me up for that. I've never been in a real earthquake before. But you wake me up for a fucking car accident. You're an asshole!"

Saying that, Wuz went back to bed and immediately fell asleep, and all was forgotten until breakfast the next morning, when she overheard others talking of the event.

So while it hasn't all been pleasant and fun and games, for the most-part, the times I spent with Sue has been an experience that I wouldn't trade for all the money in the world. She was more than a friend--much more. I guess soul mates for eternity would be the right description.

SOME GEMS SUBMITTED by Eric Armit in the UK

🏆 Jerry Quarry came over to the U.K. and was fighting a clumsy and plodding foe named Jack (middle name illegible Bodell), the British heavyweight champ. The fight started, and after looking Jack over for a few seconds, Quarry suddenly threw one punch which put Jack down and out in under a minute.

🏆 Jack was a big strong but limited fighter. He was a farmer and tended to be lost for any sensible question to ask over a fight that had been over so quickly. Finally one guy asked: "Jerry, did you find him awkward?". A dumb question in view of what had happened. Quarry paused for a couple of second and said, "Well, he fell awkwardly."

🏆 We had a heavyweight here named Stan McDermott. Stan had a leaky defense but he had a big punch so he had no great future, but the crowds loved to watch him. However, he was not the brightest guy you could ever meet. In one fight Stan had his gum shield knocked out in a neutral corner, but came right back and floored his opponent in the other neutral corner. As the ref picked up the count, Stan started trying to pick up his gum shield from the canvas, but with his gloves on every time he tried to grip it the mouthpiece jumped forward out of his grasp. Meanwhile the opponent had made it to his feet at the count of nine, but was swaying against the ropes obviously ready for the taking. The referee stepped back expecting Stan to come flying in and finish the fight only to turn around and find Stan still pursuing his gum shield around the corner. The crowd was hysterical, but Stan was set on getting his gum shield and both the ref and the opponent looked on in amazement until he finally picked up the mouthpiece and despite it being covered in resin stuck it back in his mouth and went over and kayoed the other guy.

🏆 Terry Downes, a future world middleweight champion, felt it was a big prospect for an easy payday when he was put in with a relatively unknown African fighter. Instead Terry lost and took a beating. That "unknown" African was Dick Tiger, from Nigeria. When asked who he wanted to fight next, Terry replied "the guy who made this match."

It's not all that great

- My friend, Beau Williford used to be a heavyweight fighter who now trains both pro and amateurs in his gym in Lafayette, Louisiana. Beau tells this story about one of his fighters named Lorenzo Boyd. In the mid 80's Beau set Boyd up with a match with a young Mike Tyson in the Catskill Mountains, where Mike trained, and was managed by Cus D'Amato. At first Boyd wanted no part of Tyson, but when he heard he'd be getting paid $15,000 he changed his mind, telling Beau "I'd beat my mama's ass for $15,000. I want the fight." As fight time approached, Boyd decided that he was going to surprise Tyson and take the fight to him. Williford told him that's not how he wanted him to fight the young man who was destined to become a world champion. Boyd turned to Beau and said, "I'm going to back that mother fucker up." To which Beau calmly replied, "If you fight that way, I'll have to get an ambulance ready to back you up."

- I can't say if it's original or not, but a long time ago, when I saw a low blow thrown, I mentioned that the guy was going for a TKO, a 'testicle knockout'.

THREE TRUE STORIES submitted by Elmo Adolph, outstanding referee:

- "I really don't know if this was amusing to anyone except the officials working that night. It was a show that was held in Biloxi, Mississippi. A boxer being introduced to fight in his debut got into the ring with NEW shoes, colorful trunks and robe. He was really dressed for the occasion. Although he did look too imposing he did appear to be ready. When the bell rang to start the 1st round he came to the middle of the ring. His opponent feigned a punch. But it caused the young fighter to turn around and run back to his corner and quit. Might have been one of the quickest fights ever.

🏆 "This actually happened in the amateurs. One night we were working some amateur bouts. The practice of checking for a boxer's cup has usually been that a referee would address the boxer in the corner and tap the protective cup area with the back of his hand. It is a simple process, easily done to ascertain that the boxer is wearing the cup as required. One of my best friends, Martin Coscino, who was a very good referee always had a habit of checking for a protective cup by touching the area lightly with the front of his hand.

On this particular night it seemed that everyone in the entire auditorium was focused on Martin as he went to the corner. For some reason Martin reached down and learned that the kid had no protective cup. The shocking thing was that Martin started feeling around (remember most amateurs just wore the small plastic cups) and searching for the cup. This proved futile. In a last attempt to find the cup, Martin grabbed a handful with nothing to protect the kid. It was funny as Martin just held onto the area and pointed for the kid to get out of the ring to get a cup."

🏆 At the 1975 National AAU Championships a boxer, Richard Rozelle of Columbus, Ohio was in center ring ready to have his hand raised for winning the 112 lb. championship. Right before the referee could raise his hand, Richard darted from the ring having a case of diarrhea. As he ran from the ring everyone was amazed that he could have fought under those conditions. And Richard later won the 1973 Nationals at 112 lbs."

It's not all that great

IN MORE RECENT TIMES, Gene Sebastian, brother of former middleweight champion Billy Soose, whom I had the honor to be chosen to author a book about, called me and wanted to know the phone number of our writer/historian Angelo Prospero. Somehow I spaced the last name and gave him the number of legendary trainer Angelo Dundee, another dear old friend.

Gene called the wrong Angelo and after telling him what a great job or writing he was doing for Ringsports.com, he really had Dundee confused, at least until he mentioned my name, which was something Angelo Dundee could easily relate to. Gene called me a few days later to tell me the funny screw-up that I had, unintentionally caused.

DEBORAH MUNCH, A great gal, a friend, and Vice President of public relations at Caesars Palace adds:

"The Caesars Palace president saw a man Para-gliding in circles above the ring, and called the Las Vegas Metro Police Department to report unusual parachute activity during one of the Riddick Bowe/Evander Holyfield showdowns in the resort's legendary outdoor arena. Little did we know that 'Fan Man' James Miller was plotting his course to land ringside, in mid-fight of the sold-out 15,000-seat arena.

Looking back, we guess that he may have been surprised to see that the ring is routinely topped with a broadcast lighting grid. There was no clear entrance from the sky. Round and round he went, looking for an angle that would let him disrupt the event. And disrupt it he did - for more than 20 minutes. He was relatively unhurt, though. After landing in Riddick Bowe's corner, he suffered blows from one of Bowe's camp security guards wielding a walkie-talkie. The assault was inaccurately attributed to a Caesars security guard in a Newsweek Magazine article.

"Caesars routinely rehearses crisis situations before special events. We had rehearsed 80 different scenarios before that fight. For example, if a brawl breaks out in the stands and three security guards are standing in a corner, two of them know right away that they are to stay where they are, and the third guard is to go to the situation. The ring announcer knows that he or she is to go to the center-ring with the special events director, myself, and the senior officer from Metro.

"Our most important job, in many scenarios, is to just keep the crowd calm (hence, the ring announcer, in the ring with a microphone). The Crisis Plan worked beautifully that evening. No one was hurt, not even our unwelcome Para-glider. I would call this an only-in-boxing' moment, except that two weeks later Miller landed atop Buckingham Palace, stark naked."

ANOTHER FUNNY STORY, this time from Rueben Lowing: "In 1993, at the Sunshine State Games in Tallahassee, Florida, Roy Jones Jr. was 13, and was expected to weigh in at 98 pounds, but instead came in at 106. Roy Jones, Sr. got into the Boys Club van and told everyone that his son didn't make weight. Roy Jr. got into the van and his dad, who was driving, looked into the rear view mirror at his son, and said, "I hope you fight King Kong!" Roy Jr. replied instantly, "So do I!" That retort made the older Jones laugh. The fighter that Jones had to fight that night was future light heavyweight champion Antonio Tarver. Jones won.

MORE FUNNY QUOTES:

- ♛ A funny quote submitted by boxing fan James W. Wayland and said by (who else) Mike Tyson, when he was asked if he had been rehabilitating his injured knee, "Confuiciously."

- ♛ This time from Steve McGuire: "He gets cut on the way to the stadium," said about Arturo Gatti.

It's not all that great

- 🏆 "The bell went ding and I went dong," was said by British middleweight Lloyd Honeyghan at the beginning of round two, before his controversial stoppage of Johnny Bumphus.

- 🏆 "When was the fight?" This was asked by Ken Norton when asked about his fight with Earnie Shavers, who knocked him out in round one.

- 🏆 "What, should I have done, written him a letter to say I was going to hit him?" This was said by Jack Dempsey on his controversial in-clinch punch against Jack Sharkey that ended the fight.

- 🏆 "If this keeps up, this guy is going to break his hand on your jaw". This was said by legendary trainer Angelo Dundee to Pinklon Thomas, in his corner, during his heavyweight fight with Evander Holyfield.

- 🏆 "No, I want a people doctor," said by Max Baer, on his deathbed, when asked if he wanted someone to call the house doctor.

- 🏆 "They must have been tough cab drivers." Uttered by Greg Haugen after his fight with Julio Cesar Chavez, in regard to his pre-fight comments on Chavez's opponents being Tijuana taxi drivers.

FROM CALIFORNIA OFFICIAL Jack Reiss: Marty Denkin was once refereeing a world title fight and a nervous promoter approached Marty and cautioned him that his fighter cuts easily, but is real tough and not to stop the fight just because he was a bleeder. Marty's poetic response to the promoter was "I've seen more bloody gashes then a gynecologist, don't worry. I won't stop this fight till it needs to be stopped."

FROM DAWN PACHECO, daughter of famed boxing doctor and commentator Ferdie.

"I spent a great deal of time over the years in Las Vegas working and helping where I could when my father was doing a show on Showtime in town. I was in my late 30's at the time, eldest child of a very Spanish father who was not altogether pleased that I was working around boxing. Not being proper for a woman and all. But I had always dogged him when it came to boxing and being engaged to Chuck Minker, the late Executive Director of the Nevada State Athletic Commission was only fuel to my fire for the sport and to spend real time with my father in his world.

"So, when dad can't be beat he falls on humor, always; usually at someone else's expense and very often at mine. I always knew he was a genius and very funny, often misunderstood by people not as quick of mind. And I always fell for it. I never questioned...he wanted something, I adored him, so I was front and center for his games.

"Now you might understand how we got to this one night. The fight was huge, celebrities abound, all the world sport press, a Don King production. I think it was a Tyson one puncher or Holyfield, but big time. The fight was over and we were (dad and I) walking to the press room. Dad was exhausted from just flying cross country, the climate change and commentating all night. So he was resting on the back of the room against a wall and told me in his *Fight Doctor* voice to march over to Don King who was standing in front of the entire press row and ask him for 2 tickets to get into the after fight party. Sucker that I am, I charged over and sort of asked with some authority for the passes. To which the very tall King started screaming at me in full voice, that he'd give them to me if he felt like it, and you all know Don with an audience he just went on and on. After my heart started beating again I explained in a low voice that

It's not all that great

if he sent his stepson Carl King to do his bidding he'd expect it done and that was the spot I was in. He melted right away schmoozed up to me, put his arm around me told the press he was just 'funnin' with me and gave me the passes.

"So I turn around to head back to dad and he was doubled up against the wall laughing so hard I thought he'd need oxygen. No apologies. Nada, just business as usual. The business of keeping himself amused whenever he's over tired or bored.

"That sounds awful to do to your child in public, but these were boxing people. Dad, if he loves you, respects you, wants to hang with you, and if he feels deeply he'd be the first one in line to give you bone marrow.

"As for me that night, I could have punched him out cold. I was furious, cursing all the way back to my car (under my breath and out of his ear shot, a given). But lo-and behold I run right into Carl King, a very old friend, and I start cursing dad up and down and he just stood there with his arm around me smiling ear to ear. Finally feeling he wasn't getting my whole anger thing, I asked what the hell he was smiling for. He leaned down to my ear and whispered so softly 'HOW WOULD YOU LIKE TO HAVE MY FATHER FOR FIVE MINUTES'? Kissed me on the cheek and walked off.

"There's a life lesson there for us all, don't ya think"?

Heard from ringside: "I had to quit boxing because I had bad hands, the referee kept stepping on them".

Round VI
Funny and True

PROMOTER ARNIE "TOKYO" ROSENTHAL adds this gem:

'Managing fighters is tough enough but managing one where there is a language barrier is even harder. Case in point: Merqui Sosa. His English is poor and my Spanish even poorer, but we usually managed to get by except for this one time. I had to explain to Merqui why I was going to be late due to my cat having a problem. In explaining, I said "Como se dice en espanol FLEAS." Merqui calmly said, "Por Favor." I said, "No, FLEAS." A little less calmly, Merqui again said," Por Favor." Once again I said, "No, FLEAS." Now he screamed "POR FAVOR". Finally I said "little cucarachas." Finally, he understood.

FROM FRED BERNS, leading promoter in the Mid West:

I had brought former NFL defensive end Ed 'Too Tall' Jones into Indiana for a fight. They put him up in a hotel in Indianapolis. They put him in the honeymoon suite, and there was a big, long, heart-shaped bed. When Ed saw that, he got excited because it was a big enough bed for him. He thought he was going to be able to sleep the night before the fight. He ended up not being able to fall asleep because he was so happy that he finally had a bed that could fit him.***

SOMETHING BILLED AS the "Fight of the Century" involving Bruce "The Mouse" Strauss vs. Wilbur "Vampire" Johnson in Indianapolis. Strauss and Johnson both got into the ring for the start of the first round. The referee, who hasn't seen either fighter fight before, was from Indiana. At the beginning of round one, they start feeling one another out. All of a sudden, Johnson lands a good punch; Strauss, to acknowledge the good punch, does a little wiggle-waggle back and forth, but is not really hurt. The referee, not knowing it's just an acknowledgement by Strauss, who was a character, stops the fight at one minute 20 seconds of the first round and declares Johnson a winner by TKO. He raises Johnson's hand as the victor. Which ended the "Fight of the Century," and the referee never worked another fight.

ANOTHER FRED BERNS story involves State Senator Ken Snyder of Indiana. Snyder, who was a good amateur fighter, and in 1972 was scheduled to try out for the U.S. Olympic team. On his property in Indiana he had an airstrip and helicopter pad. He gets ready that night to go to the Olympic trials. He wins the three-round fight in Indiana, and when he flies back home, on election night, he finds out that he had won the election although never even campaigning, and can no longer go on to represent the U.S. in the Olympics. Sugar Ray Seales from Tacoma, Washington, ends up taking Snyder's spot on the Olympic team. Ken Snyder goes on to become a U.S. Senator from Indiana and turned pro at age 48, for Berns, and is currently undefeated as a pro.

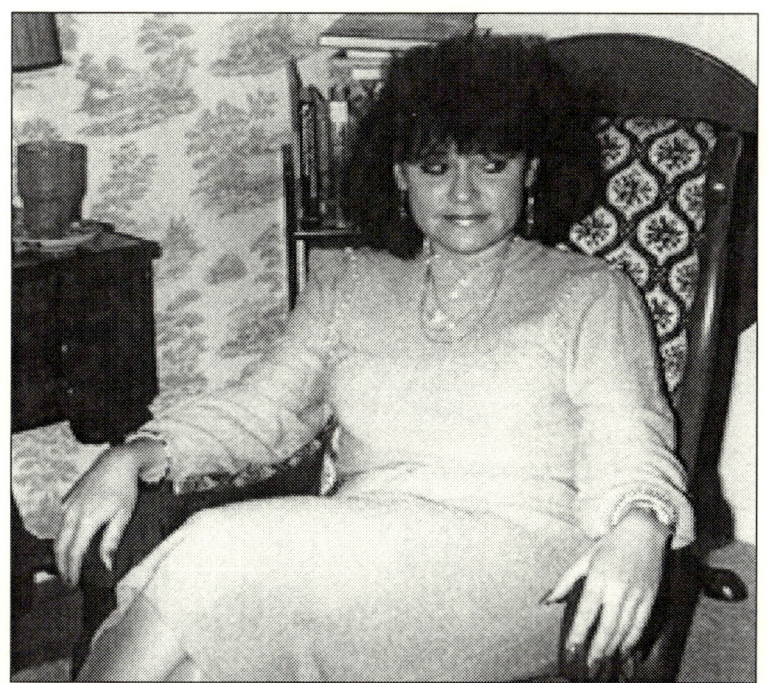
Formal Woozel

with Gil Clancy

with Freddie Little

with Gene Fullmer

with God impersonator

with Danny Wambolt
of World Boxing Hall of Fame

Bobo Olsen with Sue

Rusty & Lois

Sue's mom, Amelia

Sue's sister Marian

Eddie Futch, World's greatest trainer

FRED BERNS WAS returning to America after taking two fighters overseas for a fight. He didn't recall the name of the airline, but the plane was a 757. All of a sudden, near Canada, one of the engines on the right side of the plane started smoking. The approximate 250 passengers quickly took notice of this. They informed the stewardess, who quickly went to tell the pilot.

Since they were in Canadian airspace, the pilot figured he'd notify the Canadian authorities. They quickly made their descent into the Montreal airport after the authorities ordered them to do so. The plane fortunately made a safe landing. All of a sudden, the Canadian authorities had surrounded the plane and told the pilot that the passengers and crew were not going to be allowed off the jet, and were all being detained by the Canadian government.

After the 250 people sat on the plane for about 3 hours, the Canadian government brought up a ladder to the plane, about 3 stories high. The passengers were allowed to come off the plane, single file. When it was Fred's turn to disembark, he started to get the shakes, and he felt like he was going to mess his pants because the ladder was wobbling badly. Once the 250 people got off the plane and they were immediately escorted to a room with chairs and a telephone. A guard was placed outside the door. After about 2 hours in the room, the guard told them they were allowed to make phone calls to their families, but they had to do it one at a time. About an hour later, the officials rolled in a cart loaded with submarine sandwiches.

Still there weren't enough subs on the cart for all the people, so while some people were making calls, the rest dove for the subs. Fred and the two fighters found themselves fifth in line after starting at the end of the line. When they got to the cart, there were no subs left.

Fred went to the door and asked the security guard why there were no more sandwiches. The official said that was all they were allotted. The official told Fred the plane was not supposed to land in Canada at all; it was an "unwelcome visitor." He also told Fred, "That's how the American government usually treats Canadians in American airports." Fred turned around and told the official, "No, that's only how we treat Canadians with AIDS."

After another hour, they all finally re-boarded the plane after the mechanics had corrected the problems and Fred and the two fighters were able to eat and returned home to Indianapolis.

HALL OF FAME PROMOTER Don Fraser is now head of the Golden State Boxers Association. He was inducted in 2005 at age 78. Before the induction, he was honored with a big event in his honor in Los Angeles. Fraser, during the event expressed his awe by saying: "I'm glad this is not a memorial."

As a public relations guy, Fraser was able to get a real lion to pose with fighter Lauro "the Lion" Salas in a fight promotion at the Hollywood Legion Stadium. The trainer got the lion out of the cage and said "Nobody move." Nobody did.

Fraser was a publicist for a Muhammad Ali (then Cassius Clay) fight in LA. En route to the press conference, Fraser stopped by a discount store and brought a badge for Ali to wear. The badge read "I am the greatest." When he fought Sonny Liston two years later, Ali proclaimed to the world that "I am the greatest." Is this how the nickname came to be?

THIS BIT OF INSIGHT comes from Krysti Rosario, a young up and comer in the world of ring announcing: I was talking to a coach named Jimmy from Boston. We were agreeing that it's a shame when a boxer has a lot of natural talent and no heart. This is his quote "I'm not a wizard, I can't give you a heart."

ODDITIES I HAVE OBSERVED during my sports-writing career:

"The Greatest," Muhammad Ali, was going to be invited on a cruise I was planning to raise money for wheelchair bound

Greg Page and Gerald McClellan. I couldn't hook up with Ali to ask him to join us, so I did the next best thing, I thought. I contacted his trainer and long time friend Angelo Dundee. Angelo just said short and to the point: "Don't ask him! He won't go! Ali can't swim and is afraid of water."

AMONG THE ODDITIES I've seen include a not to be named boxing scribe knocking the hat off Bert Sugar at a Las Vegas pre-fight buffet. The event almost turned to fisticuffs.

TOUGH FORMER HEAVYWEIGHT contender George Chuvalo, when learning that he was given a star on the Toronto Canada Walk of Fame: "I'll be the first athlete there that can't skate."

FROM BOXING GURU Dan Sisneros: While I can't think of anything that outrageously funny, I do remember once when I worked as a Judge for a fight in Albuquerque. It was a fight between a local brawler named Anthony Ayon taking on an unbeaten prospect named Trey Harris in a 4 rounder. I scored it 40-36 (4 rounds to 0) for Ayon, as he just battered Harris, and pushed him all over the ring.

At the end of the fight Harris' eye was black and swollen, and almost closed, he was a bloody mess! The two other Judges had it 40-36 for Harris and 40-38 for Harris. When we went to the offices to get paid for the night's work, the agent for the promoter (Cameron Dunkin) came in and really let me have it! He said that I must be blind or drunk, or crazy to have given that fight to Ayon!!! I said that Ayon won the fight and that's all there was to it!

He responded: "Watch, the next person that comes through that door, we'll ask and you'll see!" I said OK. The door open and in walked the sports editor for the Albuquerque Tribune, John O'Rourke. Cameron asked him, "John, who won that fight between Harris and Ayon?" O'Rourke said, "Ayon dominated

Funny and True

the fight, I don't know what fight the OTHER judges were watching, but it wasn't THAT ONE!" Cameron just froze, and looked at me, then looked back at O'rourke and said... "You must be blind too!" and walked out of the office.

FROM WRITER JOHNNY WILDS, who, after watching the Jim Gray interview with Kostya Tszyu after he beat Julio Cesar Chavez in 2000, when Gray asked about the low blows, said, "Well, Jim he kept hitting me in the balls." Talk about your profound statements.***

I DON'T HAVE A LOT OF MEMORIES of my youth, but I know that I was a bit of a hellion, and drank a bit more than I should at times. Drinking the same thing all night never bothered me, (straight up of course) but whenever I would mix drinks it always had a negative effect on me.

I recall one Christmas Eve, standing outside on a street corner with my full beard, wearing a white sheet, having a crown of something that resembled thorns and holding the bible in one hand, and preaching to everyone who would listen. "The Lord says that it is far better for us to give than to receive, so give me." I didn't make any money (didn't expect to), but was fortunate that the men in the white jackets didn't pick me up.

Another time, I walked out of a bar, and into what I thought was a taxi cab and told the driver (a police officer) to take me home. Wrong car, the cab was next in line. The officer politely refused me. And I thought he was supposed to be a public servant. Shows what I knew.

I recall driving a cab in New York for a short time to earn some extra cash, and a guy walked out of a bar, into one door of the cab and right out the other, then told me it was a great ride and we really got there quickly and threw me a ten dollar bill.

THERE HAVE BEEN A FEW husband and wife teams in boxing, it began, at least to the best of my recollection, with the late ring announcer Frank Shain and his late wife, Judge Eva Shain of New Jersey.

Currently we have referee Robert Byrd and his wife judge Adelaide of Nevada, and also in Nevada, awaiting work is former referee/judge Tony Castellano and active judge, his wife Carol. Tony has refereed over 100 world title fights and Carol more than 30.

Like Frank and Eva Shain, Tony and Carol have blessed this scribe with their friendship.

While Eva Shain judged a world title bout aboard an aircraft carrier in Florida, Carol Castellano was the first woman judge to work a title fight in England. And another good friend, Gwen Adair, was the first female referee. About time the fairer sex got an equal opportunity.

MORE EXPERIENCES AND quotes, including, Larry Holmes on Don King: "I made more money with him stealing from me than I would have with any other promoter."

Top amateur coach Bobby Lee chimes in: "Show me a good loser and I'll show you a loser."

MORE LOU DUVA STORIES from Florida based trainer Gus Curran. "In 1996, when I opened the House of Champions Gym, me and Lou and David Tua were eating lunch together, and Lou jokingly makes a remark to David about being dumb. He said 'David, you're so slow it takes you an hour and a half to watch 'Sixty Minutes".

Gus, Duva and heavyweight Mike Marrone were in Washington, D.C. Curran explains: "Lou wants to show us around so we hail a cab. The driver is of Middle Eastern descent, and hard for us to understand. Every time the driver says anything, Lou responds with the word *si*. The driver cracks up laughing and says, 'You think I'm Spanish?' And

Lou responds. 'I don't know what the hell you are, but you're taking the long way to the monument."

CURRAN RECALLS ANOTHER time: "Lou walks into my gym and my English Bulldog Bruno is there and Bruno slowly walks over to him. They are both staring at each other. Lou says, 'Is this your dog?' I reply "Yeah." Lou says: "I like him, he looks like me." They really do look like each other and now, when Lou comes to my house or the gym, Bruno gets up and sits right on Lou's foot."

FROM MARC RATNER, renowned ex-Executive Director of the Nevada. State Athletic Commission: 'One quick story off the top of my head. In December of 1989 Ray Leonard fights Roberto Duran, at the Mirage. About 10 minutes before they walk out to the ring, in Duran's dressing room he says something in Spanish to his wife. She leaves for a minute and brings back an empty bottle into the dressing room. Roberto has his gloves on, she has to help get his trunks and cup off and has to hold and aim Roberto's urine into the bottle. I haven't seen anything like that in all my years in boxing and I was certainly hoping that he didn't miss. Fortunately, he didn't.

MOST OF MY MEMORIES in dealing with boxing people have been positive and often fun. Some are as follows:

Bobby and Jean Lee of Hawaii are two great folks who have done much to promote our sport. I am proud to call them both friends.

Bobby's biggest claim to fame was that he stopped the Muhammad Ali/Trevor Berbick fight from happening in Oahu, where it was originally scheduled for. Ali was finished (the fight vs. Berbick in the Carribean proved that) and him being in the ring was an accident waiting to happen. It took courage to say no to the great Ali, but Lee, a native of Hawaii and a child survivor of Pearl Harbor has never been accused of not having the courage of his convictions.

ANOTHER FRIEND THAT I made in the sport was Jorge Paez, a two-time world champion, a great guy who has done a lot to promote the sport. Jorge has a great sense of humor. At a press conference a number of years back, I told Jorge that I visit his hometown (Mexicali) on occasion. He smiled and said, "Next time you come and visit with me." I asked him if he was in the telephone book and he replied, "No, but no problem finding me, amigo. Just ask the Fedarales, they always know how to find me."

Some years later Paez was standing in line behind me and Wuz at the Eldorado Hotel and Casino buffet. A friend who was going to comp us the dinner and was supposed to have the comps at the register, had apparently forgotten, and as I reached for my wallet to pay for it, Jorge stopped me and said to the cashier, 'just put in on my bill. Paez was doing radio commentary for the event. Jorge Paez is probably best remembered for shaving his head with messages like "Say no to drugs" or wearing outlandish costumes into the ring.

HERE'S AN ODDITY sent in by Steve Turkish: "I grew up a sports fan in Brooklyn, NY in the 60's. I watched the Yankees, Mets, and Knicks like every other kid in New York. One night when I was about 14 years old, my parents were going out for the night. I looked at the newspaper and saw that the only sports event on television was the George Chuvalo/Dante Cane fight. I remember watching from the living room television as Chuvalo beat this guy from Italy and this was my first taste of boxing. I loved it and became a huge boxing fan. I've since traveled around the country and have seen hundreds of fights.

This (2005) February, I was at the Orleans Hotel in Las Vegas watching the fights. I started talking with the guy sitting next to me. He said he was from Toronto. We talked about fighters from years ago and he said the first fight he ever went to was the Chuvalo/Cane fight at Maple Leaf Gardens with his dad. He was amazed when I told him the first fight I ever saw also was that fight, even if it was on TV. What are the chances of that happening?"

ON A PERSONAL NOTE, I've met various fighters over the years and had a few fun confrontations at press conferences.

Ray Mancini, in exchange to a question he seemed not to like, asked if I wanted to step outside. I refused.

Roberto Duran under similar circumstances threatened to get jailed Panamanian President Noriega after me.

And in one of the classics, Leon Spinks, when I asked what strategy he would employ against Dwight Muhammad Qawi, just look up and sang (sort of) nah, nah nah nah nah, I'm not gonna tell you.

MORE INTERESTING QUOTES AND EVENTS:

"I'm not saying I was robbed, but has anybody seen my wallet?" Bernard Hopkins after losing a close, controversial decision to Jermain Taylor.

NORTHERN NEVADA AMATEUR official Don Kennedy tells of the time he refereed a fight in Virginia City, and the fighter threw up twice on the ring. Always looking out for the health and welfare of the fighter, Don stopped the fight, and in his way of saying thanks, the fighter took a swing at him. (He missed).

VETERAN LAS VEGAS boxing Commissioner and Judge Art Lurie adds these two gems: \One took place in the Olympic Auditorium in Los Angeles, when "Kingfish" Levinsky took on

"Slapsy" Maxie Rosenbloom. Max, who hardly knocked anyone down, let alone out cold, threw an overhand right which sent Levinsky to the canvas. Rosenbloom was so surprised by the knockdown that he actually laid down on the mat beside Levinsky and took an 8-count with him."

The second bit of humor also took place in L.A., between Glenn Lee and Abbie Miller. Miller's brother, who also managed him, was a friend of Lee's manager, Joey Greenberg. The contest, which was scheduled for 10-rounds, ended abruptly in the sixth, when Lee knocked Miller out. At that point, more than 50 angry fight fans jumped into the ring and a free-for-all occurred. As a result of this riot, the FBI apprehended one of the 10 most wanted men in the country. The guy got so carried away with the mob that he jumped into the ring to join in. A picture of the scene was printed in the L.A. Times, and the FBI was able to locate and apprehend a long sought after criminal.

RINGSPORTS.COM WRITER LARRY Tornambe may be the only reporter punched at ringside during a fight, by one of the boxers! While at ringside, covering a fight at the Legendary Blue Horizon, Larry witnessed a heavyweight boxer swing and miss and hurled his upper body over the top rope. The boxer's feet remained inside the ropes, but his gloves were on the ring apron, his body held up by the top rope, which also threatened to slide up and press on his throat.

Being over 240 pounds, the referee couldn't straighten the boxer, the fighter was stuck in the jackknife position and all this was going on directly in front of Larry. Tornambe reached up to the fighter's shoulders, to push his upper body up far enough so he and the ref could straighten the poor guy out. When Larry pushed the boxer's shoulders up, his gloves came off the ring apron and his right hand clunked Larry on the side of the head. Larry was unhurt and, unfortunately, it was the boxer's best punch of the night as he lost a decision.

ICEMAN JOHN SCULLY former high level contender, writes: "I have always liked the Gym and the banter that goes on there on a given day. Sometimes little rivalries develop. Sometimes guys argue about who is going to win an upcoming big fight or sometimes you have two amateur kids in the gym about to meet up in a tournament and the gym is divided on who the winner will be. Sometimes there is heated sparring going on and it can get personal with everybody in the gym egging the two boxers on. Sometimes the gym can get very personal to the point of blows being exchanged outside the ring. I've seen that a few times. I've even been directly involved in the action on occasion. Stuff like that. Sometimes there is funny dialogue, too.

Scully continues: Back around 1994 I was in the Gym sparring with my good friend Vinny Paz and afterwards, as usual, we hung out for a while and talked Boxing or whatever. Sometimes over the past few years I had come to spar and by chance I would have my Roy Jones T-Shirt on and sometimes the conversation would turn to Roy. I had sparred with both Vinny and Roy at that point many times already and could probably lay claim to being someone that could say they knew both guys very well inside the four ropes.

Vinny respected Roy a lot as a champion with skills but sometimes Kevin Rooney, Vinny's trainer, wouldn't be as impressed. Kevin is a Cus D'Amato disciple and I always got the impression that all the speed and flash didn't impress him very much. So, anyway, the three of us sat down that day at the round table in Vinny's gym and when I started talking good about Roy, Kevin got real animated as he sometimes does and started waving his hands saying "You know. You're always talking about Jones. Jones this, Jones that. Lemme' ask ya' something... who hits harder, Roy Jones or Vinny?!?"

I remember having the obvious feeling of being put on the spot. I am in the middle--Kevin to my left and my friend Vinny two feet away to my right. I am honest about my boxing opinions/feelings and I am not one to lie just to sound good to who I am talking to. I looked at Kevin (he had a disgusted look on his face), then at Vinny (he knew what I was going to say), then back at Kevin.

"Well... Roy hits harder than Vinny. I was kind of quiet and even tempered with Kevin as I always respected him from when I first met him as a sixteen year old in 1983 when he had Tyson at the Gloves in Holyoke, Mass.

He twisted his face up at my response, though, and brushed me off with a wave of his hand and said "Ahhh, you don't know what you're talking about. You never been hit by him then." I still respect Kevin and we have been friendly together since that day, but for the next moment I became the real ME and I was talking to just some guy and not the famous Kevin Rooney. I said "What?? Man, YOU have never been hit by him. You don't know what your talking about because if YOU had been hit by him you wouldn't be sitting here having this conversation!"

That pretty much ended the debating part of our conversation.

MORE STORIES, FUNNY and otherwise:
With thanks to Ryan Wissow, a guy named Jeff Love needed an opponent. Jeff lost all his fights and needed a "win." Eventually he got his cousin to fight him. His cousin had never been in a gym or ever had a pair of gloves on in his life. Of course, having absolutely no boxing experience and being off the street, he owned no boxing equipment. He needed a foul guard (cup) for his fight with Jeff. So one of the prelim fighters lent him his foul guard, still soaking in sweat from the last fight. The cousin then turned around, put the foul guard on his HEAD, thinking it was a headgear, and was trying to figure out how to fasten it! This was a pro fight and of course they don't allow headgear. So after all this, the cousin went out there and KO'd Jeff in the 1st round.

James W. Wayland submits this true story. It isn't very politically correct but here goes: Georgie Benton telling Evander

Holyfield that he would be the "deadest nigger in the cemetery" if he allowed George Foreman to land his big right hand."

California ref Marty Sammon contributes thusly: "San Quentin Cal. fighters weren't doing much, action wise, and from the stands came the taunt "turn off the lights, they want to be alone."

From Glen Hamada, world renowned boxing judge from Washington: Here is a story that I remember about a boxing match that took place at Charley Mac's Bar and Casino in Washington about 10 years ago. I cannot remember the boxers, however, this story is funny.

The inspectors of the fight as well as the referees failed to inspect the ring ropes. The judges were myself, Tom McDonough and Barry Druxman. During the first round, these two heavyweights were grabbing and holding and not punching very much. The fight was more of a sumo match as these two fighters did more pushing, shoving and holding/hitting. As the fight progressed into the third round, both fighters were wrestling each other and one boxer was pushed over the top of the loose ring rope directly onto Barry Druxman. Barry was flattened by the heavyweight as Barry weighed only about 130 lbs. Barry was shaken, but like a true warrior he got up and finished scoring the bout.

From good friend Robert Quam, D.C. My fighter Rick Rogers, a great natural talent, got good enough in 1967 or thereabouts to spar with Mando Ramos. This was at Jake Shugrues gym in Los Angeles. I remember it was a Saturday morning. He and Mando were sparring in one of Shugrues rings. Mando, being Mando, was popping him pretty good, so I told him to tie Mando up, which he did, but Mando (the greatest natural talent I ever saw in person) hit him anyway. Rick just glared at me. What could one say? It was Mando Ramos for petes sake.

Another time at the legendary Herman Newman gym in San Francisco, I walked into the gym and saw Elmer Rush, an army champion, who turned pro and who had gone with me to Fort Ord, Monterey, California, where I had and won my first fight. Elmer was sparring with some big bruiser, and saw me. He turned his head to nod hi and the guy clocked him. Rush almost went down.

Round VII
Woozel Bwain

IT WAS IN THE EARLY 80's and I had kept Susiey Walker around me, not just because she was my best friend, but because she was naturally one of the funniest (and strangest) gals I have ever known. Laughing is good for the soul, and is supposed to help you live longer, but in Sue's case, the latter proved untrue, as she got colon cancer in 1989, and her demise was only five years later.

Having Wuz around did help me to relax, although I almost always had to be on my toes when we were together, trying to figure out what goofy thing she would do next. Sue was every bit as unpredictable as the Northern Nevada weather.

One summer, shortly after I had separated from my ex-wife, Sue, I, and my kids drove to a lake in Northern California to picnic and go paddle-boating. Sue gave one of my kids a dollar to pull my bathing shorts down in front of all the people at the crowded beach. Not like it was something she hadn't seen before, but at the time, it seemed like a fun thing for her to do, and I guess my kids enjoyed it also, but it probably scared the hell out of all the onlookers.

This was a very rough time in my life, financially, as I was out of work. but Sue would come over to my studio apartment a couple of times a week, bringing inexpensive food like spaghetti and potatoes, some of her home-baked goodies (Wuz was a great cook, as is her sister, Marion) and always a full bag of the local newspapers that her mom subscribed to, so I could keep informed.

Not that I couldn't afford a newspaper, but, truth be told, even that could be marginal at times, and I wasn't then and still am not a big fan of the local rag. This was one of the few times that I was completely out of boxing, and I was really hurting for money, but Sue was always there for me, and I never had to ask for her help. I rarely would ask her for any financial help, but I know that she would have provided what she could, had I done so. And she knew that she would get it back.

If I was not at home, Sue always had the key to the apartment and would leave the bag(s) of goodies on the table inside. In many ways, up to when I married Lois, Wuz had become the best thing that had ever happened to me, because no matter how bad things were going for me at the time, she always was able to get me to laugh without trying. Sometimes Sue even did things that would upset me, but very seldom.

ONE NIGHT SHE CAME over to my studio and wanted me to go with her to the nearby Comstock Hotel Casino to play Keno. That evening, no matter how much we tried, and believe me we were so tired at the end, we really tried hard, she couldn't lose her money, so having had quite a few drinks, and as usual refusing to spend the night with me, she drove home about 3AM. Three hours later she returned, bright eyed and bushy tailed, and woke me up, telling me that she couldn't sleep and wanted to go to Circus Circus, another casino, to eat breakfast, have a few drinks and play some more Keno. Sue knew that I could never refuse her anything, and although I had a blazing headache (hangover), we did have a lot of fun.

Another time Wuz picked me up in the morning, telling me that she knew of 'a great secluded spot, near a lake, where we could get it on'. She found the 'familiar' spot quickly. And it was totally deserted at the time, probably because it had little sand and was pretty rocky. We put down the blanket, managed to get undressed and started to get it on. Soon Sue, who was positioned underneath me, tapped me on the shoulders and pointed to about a half dozen people who were staring at us. I was too far gone to stop, so all I could do is turn to them and yell, "I hope you guys are enjoying the show." Sue had managed to find this "great secluded spot" that just happened to be a *boat landing*. I should have known better. Sue had absolutely no sense of direction.

I remember a time, getting even (real revenge) with Sue for some of her practical jokes, when I put a couple of small bottles of sunscreen oil in her body lotion. We were in Vegas and I knew how much she loved to sit around the pool and get a tan. She would never use any sunscreen, which I felt was foolish, so I discretely put the sunscreen in the lotion and it took Sue three days to figure out why, no matter how much she sat in the hot sun, she wasn't getting a tan. Hey, revenge can be sweet.

I once accompanied Wuz to the county courthouse to pay a parking ticket. After she had made the transaction, as an afterthought, she jokingly asked the cashier if she could get any drink tokes (free drink tickets) with the payment. You have to live in a gambling city to appreciate that bit of humor. To our great surprise, the cashier said, "wait a minute," turned around, went to her desk, and returned with a handful of drink tokes, saying that her son would only find and use them and he drinks enough already.

In the early to mid eighties, (it was still a number of years before I met my wife to be, Lois), Sue was the gal of choice and the only gal for me. I admit to being more then just a bit obsessed by her, but it wasn't mutual in that respect. It was to be a great, long lasting friendship, which ultimately wound up with Wuz being my soul mate, nothing more. But she will remain my soul mate through eternity and that in itself is saying a lot.

Wuz had owned two Ford Pintos that her son had borrowed, and subsequently wrecked, fortunately without any serious injury to himself or others, and Sue finally wound up with a white Mitsubishi, through her husband Jack, which she washed and waxed as often as possible, and treasured until the very end. She ordered and placed a "JINX" license plate on the vehicle. That car was her pride and joy, and her son Dorian was not allowed to drive it (although he did the few times he could get away with it.. Because my car was an older gas hog, the Mitsubishi was the vehicle that Sue and I took most of our trips to Northern California in.

Sue was diagnosed with colon cancer in 1999, as a result of her bad habit of always putting things off. She was a world class procrastinator. Wuz figured that her rectal bleeding that was ongoing for more than a month was caused by hemorrhoids, and by the time she visited the doctor, she discovered that it was a polyp that had turned to cancer. No one had realized how much she was bleeding; if they did they would have pushed her to see a doctor much earlier. By the time she finally saw the doctor it was far too late to do any good.

However, she was always a fighter, and kept living her life one day at a time, for as long as she could, to the fullest. Sue was the main reason that I started Glove2Glove and the prayers that have, over the years, come in for her, and many others, has become my main source of giving back to boxing. Perhaps it will be Glove2Glove, rather than my writings, that will ultimately go down as my legacy to boxing.

I clearly remember the Wednesday evening that Wuz called me, very upset, and told me that the doctor told her that "It didn't look good." I could have gone to the doctor with her that day, and certainly would have, if I had any inkling of the seriousness of the matter, but I was playing bridge and figured, as she did, that it was something minor.

I did accompany her to the surgeon who gave her a choice of treatments, radiation and chemotherapy, or surgery, none offered anything close to a guarantee. I'll never forget Sue turning to the doctor after giving her the choices, saying "You mean I'm going to die". That simple, innocent remark took an awful lot out of me. Sue of course opted for the chemo because she was much too vain to wear a colostomy bag.

ONE HUMOROUS INCIDENT that I readily recall took place in Las Vegas. Keep in mind that Sue could never find her way out of a paper bag on a bright sunny day. Right after we arrived at my timeshare, Wuz decided to go for her regular walk (she was always on a diet and into health) and two mile walks were commonplace for her at the time). Our room was on the top (third) floor at the far end of the hallway.

Wuz said I shouldn't worry, that she was a big girl and knew *exactly* where our room was, and left for her half-hour walk, which quickly turned into more than an hour. Sue finally returned to our room, a bit red-faced, and not just from the hot Vegas sun. Seems like when she got back to the timeshare, she correctly went to the third floor and the far end of the hall, the *opposite* end, and when some guy on the other side of the door she knocked on asked who it is, she replied: "Come on you fucking pussy, open the damn door." I can only imagine the expression on her face when a trembling small guy, who looked to her to be about 90 years old, slowly complied. Of course, realizing her error, Wuz immediately apologized.

Sue would just as frequently even get lost in Reno, (and she lived here for more than 30 years) and often had to rely on landmarks to get to where she was going. The only time Wuz was never late was when we had a trip to go on, and she certainly didn't want to miss the flight. I clearly remember running through various airports, doing my best O.J. Simpson impression, on more than one occasion. Sue loved to travel. Even to the last weeks of her life, she was busy planning our next trip.

Why was she constantly late on all the other occasions? Wuz explained it to me this way, usually at a doctor's office or other important appointment, while I was patiently waiting for her to show up to: "The doctors always keep me waiting, so why shouldn't I keep them waiting?" This was Woozel logic to the max. Besides, the fact remained that the doctors did have emergencies to deal with, she failed to comprehend (or care). And doctors were not the only ones she was constantly late for, as I was in the hospital emergency rooms and other locations waiting for her as well.

WITHOUT A DOUBT, the funniest thing Sue did, certainly not on purpose, and which was the weirdest thing that I've ever seen in my entire life, (wish I had had a camcorder with me) was at the timeshare in Vegas. I was coming out of the shower when I heard Sue screaming at the top of her lungs. I ran out to see what the problem was, and there she was, sitting on the bed, a battery powered hand mixer sticking out of her hair, and she was looking up at it cross eyed, and screaming. It would have made first prize for life on "America's Favorite Home Videos" (if anyone would ever have believed someone could do this by accident). This was truly a moment to remember.

I couldn't stop laughing as I dropped the towel, and wound up on the floor with tears coming out of my eyes, as she continued to scream and curse at me to remove the dreaded item. I got up and immediately saw that it would take less than 15 seconds to get it out of her hair, but of course I wasn't going to let it go that easily. I couldn't resist telling Wuz that it was badly tangled, and I'd have to find a scissors to use. This of course set off another round of screaming and cursing, and she, in no uncertain terms, told me that if I cut her hair, she wouldn't leave the room until it grew back, or until we were ready to return to Reno. While the thought of seeing Sue this way for a week was very tempting, I had my fun and decided to calm her down, and quickly removed the device.

Why did she do it? Yes, I asked. While I was taking the shower Sue decided that her scalp was itchy, and that the mixer was a good device to use to massage it with. And why did she pack the hand mixer? Because, always weight conscious, she took along a can of powdered Slim Fast that she intended to mix and drink in the room.

You'd think she would have learned, but Wuz was determined to do goofy things, because only she would think that they weren't goofy at all, but perfectly natural. And to Sue, they were.

A few years later, I had married Lois, and we had Sue watching our house when we went on a trip. She did exactly the same with my very heavy massager (thumper), and wound up actually to actually cutoff some of her hair. I wish I would have seen that one, as she told me she was running around the house trying to find a scissors, with my dogs, thinking she was playing with them, running after her and barking. This time she actually learned, because it took quite some time and a permanent before she felt comfortable enough to leave the confines of her home.

I recall another incident when Sue was watching the house, and went to pick Lois and me up at the airport, before returning to her home. It was during the daylight hours and Wuz wore nothing but a shear pink nightgown, with a few noticeable holes in it, and absolutely nothing underneath. I asked her about it but she never explained and out of fear of hearing the explanation, I let the subject drop.

SUE, WHEN WE FIRST MET, loved her 'serenity'. But towards the end of her life she didn't want to be alone, and with the constant fear of death lingering, that's certainly very understandable.

She loved relaxing in hot tubs and to travel out of town with me for getaways that would last from three days to two weeks. Towards the end, she became much too week for any real travel, so I spent most of my time with her at her home. She had lost a lot of weight and could hardly get out of bed.

Another Woozel thing was always watching her weight. She always seemed to have a diet book on her, where she would take note of all the calories and fat grams she consumed with each meal.

I recall another time when we flew to Vegas, and I couldn't help but notice how heavy her luggage was. She was on another of her health kicks, and had me bring along my pressure cooker, but that wasn't in *her* luggage. It was in mine! Being afraid to hear her answers, I didn't immediately ask why her luggage was so heavy.

When we picked up our luggage in Vegas, a boxing friend Stu, picked us up at the airport, and when we lifted Sue's luggage to put into his van, he grew pale. "What the fuck do you have in here?" he asked, pointing to the expandable luggage. Since Sue had told me on the plane, what she had brought along with her, I just shrugged and told him that he really didn't want to know.

But Stu insisted, "I *do* want to know", so I turned to Wuz: "You tell him". She did. Besides a full case of Slim Fast in cans, she had purchased a lot of frozen lamb chops that she got on sale, and that still frozen, she wrapped in aluminum foil, and that had remained still encased in ice, which explained all of the extra weight.

IN THE MID EIGHTIES, our hangout, Karl's Silver Club ran a contest, a drawing for a trip to a surprise location and there would be three couples winning a trip to one of three surprise destinations. The proviso, besides entering the contest, was to come to the drawing with your bags packed. I told Sue the truth, that I had a very strong feeling that I was going to win, and although her mother laughed at me, Sue convinced her to humor me, and she wisely came to the drawing with her bags packed.

We won a trip to Southern California for three days, including a chauffeured limousine from the casino to the airport. There was no cash involved (nor promised) but a car rental would have been a nice and valuable add on, not that it was bad just having one of the winning tickets. When they reached into the barrel, pulled and announced my name as the second winner (there were thousands of entries, and twice as many people on hand, or so it seemed) I walked downstairs to draw an envelope as to where the trip would be going and it turned out to be the Red Lion Hotel in Ontario, California.

Sue was shocked. While I headed downstairs to claim my prize, Sue turned to my friend Phil and asked "What do I do now?" Phil provided Wuz with a simple answer: "Go and enjoy yourself." When I drew the envelope with the surprise trip in it, the guy who did the announcing for the event asked who I was going to be taking with me. The gal, a friend who handled the Silver Club's PR, who was co-hosting the drawing chimed in, "Susiey of course." Like it was ever a deep, dark secret.

Since there was no rental car provided, and I had some cash but no credit card on hand, we took two buses to get to Disneyworld. At the time, car rentals required major credit cards, (I assume they still do). We had fun, but a problem arose when we were ready to head back to our hotel in Ontario, and we found that the buses stopped running to Riverside (where we would change over to a bus back to the Red Lion) after 6 PM. Who would have thought that buses from a major resort would stop running to a major interchange early? Certainly not me. Sue got angry, and hit me with every other man she knew would have found out when the buses stopped running. It didn't help when I told her that every other man she knew were losers and would steal from her.

So we had to spend the night in a small, run down hotel near Disneyworld, and returned to the hotel the next day, with Wuz still angry.

While we were at Disneyworld, Sue dared me to go on the roller coaster with her. It was called "The Matterhorn." I never really cared much for roller coasters, but I don't get motion sickness unless it's on a full stomach and even then it would be unusual.

We waited in a long line (everything seemed to have long lines there) and Wuz started to get antsy. It seemed like, to her surprise that she, not me, was the one who was fearful of the ride. A nice young couple behind us heard the conversation and calmed her down by saying they would share the car with us. Having no way out except to admit her fear, which she would never do in front of others, Sue got on the ride with me. The entire ride she was sitting behind me, holding on to my neck and yelling like everyone else and seemingly having a great time. When we got off the ride she looked at me and said, "That was really scary, wasn't it?" I looked at her and said: "Why are you asking me? You were on the same ride I was?" Without batting an eye, Sue looked at me and replied: "I know, but my eyes were closed the entire time."

Shortly after we returned from the Disneyworld trip, I was doing a restaurant review in a Mexican establishment in Carson City, and of course Wuz was with me, as my assistant. She was supposed to have at least a working knowledge, at least, of Mexican cuisine, but while talking about the establishment to the owners, she ordered "flutos." The owner looked up, startled, and Sue kicked me under the table, her old standby. Thinking quickly, I told the owner of our recent trip to Southern California, and that Wuz meant flautas, not flutos, which obviously were two dogs from Disneyworld.

THERE CAME A TIME when Wuz accompanied me to the grand opening of the new Ormsby House parking garage in Carson City. There was a little gathering, with cake and champagne, and as expected Sue had more than her share of the bubbly. I had to go to the restroom, and asked Sue to hold my paper plate holding the soft and moist chocolate cake. When I returned, I sat down, on the mushy cake, which Sue had put on my seat to "reserve" it. We had to leave quickly, before someone thought I had an accident. Of course Sue wouldn't leave without a final glass of champagne, and feeling no pain, asked the cocktail waitress for another drink. Instead of "excuse me, miss" or "excuse me ma'am," she came out with *"excuse me mess."* Such were the adventures of life with a Woozel.

Woozel, Boxing and Me

I readily recall sitting in a bar at the Silver Club, with Wuz, waiting for our first drink. We both knew Audrey, the female bartender pretty well. She told us that she was very upset since her dog had died during the evening, in its sleep. Without a thought, Sue responded: "Do you mean to say that your dog just woke up dead?" A true Woozel question.

Sue had always maintained a strange variety of friends, and while I have no reason to name any of them here, they were, for the most part, so far beneath her in intelligence and street smarts that I don't know where she ever found them, let alone why she kept them. Maybe it was her martyr complex.

One of her gal friends was very slow, couldn't hold any job, and resorted to whatever she had to in order to survive. If it meant stealing or selling her body, so be it. This gal drank and smoked heavily, even though she had recently witnessed both of her parents dying of cancer.

Wuz did have at least one fairly normal friend besides me. This gal lived in Carson City, and except for a few problems including gambling, seemed like a very nice person. However, before Sue got very ill, her friend's gambling (and Sue's inability to say no) caused Wuz a few unneeded health problems, like a grand mal seizure. Sue, who had a very hard time saying no to her 'friends', would hang out with her, even though her gambling would keep Sue up all night, lowering her weakened resistance even more.***

About six months after Sue passed away, I had eaten lunch with her older sister, Marian at a local Greek restaurant. After some reminiscing and a few tears, Marian went back to work, and I got into my car to return home to the keyboard (computer, not piano). I had no idea that my wife had changed the station earlier and when I flipped on the car radio. The first two songs they played were Ray Charles "Georgia on my Mind" Sue's favorite and then "My Way" by Frank Sinatra, which was and still is my favorite song.

Someone upstairs, maybe Sue herself, had this set-up rigged.

TO BE QUITE HONEST, I consider just about everyone I've met in the boxing community a friend. We're in one of the toughest businesses and in a sport that probably gets less respect than any of the others, yet, to a man (or woman) they are some of the finest people on this Earth.

LEE SAMUELS, PUBLICIST for Top Rank is one of the nicest guys around.

The late Jack Welsh, a boxing and sports writer for many years, long maintained a great sense of humor despite the unbelievable hours he would put into his craft. I don't think he ever slept, and he was in his late 70's. Maybe it's the work that kept him going.

The late Jay Edson, who was a great boxing "front man" and who also had been involved as a referee in our sport as well as active in other sports. He was a "Super guy." He was the man who worked for White Sox head honcho, Chuck Cominsky, and who came up with the idea of signing midget Eddie Gaedel to use as a pinch hitter.

The list goes on and on, and no matter how I try, I know I'll forget a lot of people to continue reminiscing in this vein. Suffice to say, I love boxing and the people in it. It has been good to me and I hope I have, in some small part, been able to return the compliment.

As for my old friend Jack Welsh, he was a well-known sports writer for many different publications and websites, including our own Ringsports.com. I knew Jack probably longer then I knew Sue, and in many ways he was every bit as goofy as she was. But in fairness, you have to be goofy to be in the boxing business, that many years. Jack had a great sense of humor.

The day he died I got a phone call from the Clark Country Coroners office telling me that Jack passed away in his sleep and had my phone number by his telephone and they didn't know who else to call. That was one story I never wanted to have to break.

SOME MORE GOOFY quotes from over the years:

- "The whale has just been harpooned," was said by HBO TV commentator Larry Merchant after Kirk Johnson was knocked down and out by Wladamir Klitschko.

- "Every weekend someone got killed in a knife fight. And if your enemies didn't get you, the police would." by George Foreman, on growing up in Houston, Texas.

- "Prizefighting gives prostitution a bad name" said by promoter Don Elbaum, in explaining why the State of Nevada didn't like the idea of boxing and brothels working in the same State.

- "I'm at a disadvantage as a promoter. I have no record of lying, stealing and cheating". Said by Lou DiBella, talking about his company, DiBella Entertainment.

- "Maybe the lesson to be learned is to be careful what you wish for" said by promoter Gary Shaw, on Bob Arums calls for an investigation into the scoring of the De la Hoya/Mosley rematch.

- "Cause I could see he was afraid of me…So I wanted him to know I'm a good guy." Mike Tyson, when asked why he left a $2.00 tip for a $1.00 ice cream cone.

- "I'm an alchemist. I can turn money into caca." Mike Tyson in talking about his poor handling of the money he had made in the ring.

- "Why are they coming at me with this (junk)? Main Events thinks I'm their Kunta Kinte." Middleweight contender Vivian Harris on his relationship with Main Events.

- "You're coming off the street to fight for the heavyweight title, and you don't want to fight? You kidding me?" IBF heavyweight champ Chris Byrd, on what he told Gerald Nobles who turned down a fight against him.

- From Eric Stevenson, a big boxing guy from Canada: 1999 Dean Storey Vs Derrick Brown, Buffalo, New York--Baby Joe Mesi undercard. I was working Dean's corner for a 4-round fight. He got caught in the first with a straight right because of his habit of dropping his left hand. Dean finished the round and I jump on him about the left. He slides through the 2nd without getting caught. In the third round he gets nailed again, does a complete back flip in the ring, and ends up in the sitting position with a great big smile on his face. The ref counts him out and myself and the Doc jump into the ring. The doc does the flashlight thing in his eyes and asks him his name--he says Dean. The doc then asks him if he knows where he is. He says yes. He is in Portland, Maine, fighting Zuri Lawrence, a fight he had a few years earlier. The Doc looks at me and knowing Dean is Canadian says, "At least he's got the right country!"

Round VIII

The High and the Flighty

I OFTEN GET ASKED about some of the experiences that I've had and the people that I've met in this sport, which is perhaps the toughest of all athletic endeavors. In short, what follows is what stands out most over my 50 plus years in boxing, as a fan, participant, sportscaster, writer, and currently editor.

I suppose my first outstanding memory and the event that first got me interested in the sport of boxing, was watching the Archie Moore/Yvonne Durelle fight from New Brunswick, Canada, in my Uncle's living room in Brooklyn, NY. True, I was very young and impressionable, but to this day, that was probably the best fight I remember seeing on Television. In fact, for pure sustained 12-round action, it still is.

Step two was when heavyweight champion Floyd Patterson regularly came to Park Place (where I lived in Brooklyn) to visit his Aunt Savannah. I had just become a teenager. What a class act Floyd was, he sparred with the kids on the block and was a perfect example of everything that was right about the sport of boxing. Sadly, Floyd is not doing well at the time of this writing, as he has a new opponent, a real killer, Alzheimer's, and the blank facial expression that he shows at times tells me that he no longer seems to remember who I am, but he was a credit to our sport, and I will always consider him a friend.

I hadn't seen or spoken with Floyd in many years when I saw him at a rules committee meeting at Bally's Casino (now the Hilton) in Reno. He was there to watch his adopted son, Tracy Harris Patterson, do battle with Lupe "Little Guns" Gutierrez. Floyd looked the same as I remembered him, time hadn't changed him physically, at least outwardly. He was pouring a cup of coffee and I walked up behind him and whispered "How's your Aunt Savannah doing?" He nearly dropped the coffee cup, turned around, remembering me right away, he said "Rusty"? and gave me a big bear hug.

I did an interview with Patterson shortly later, and I told him of the problems that my best friend Sue was having with her son, Dorian, who was continuing to have major problems with alcohol and drugs. He asked for Dorian's address. When he returned to his home in New Paltz, New York, he wrote Dorian a beautiful letter, encouraging the young man to find a better way of life. Unfortunately, Dorian was not about to listen or respond to anyone, at least not at that point in his young life.

The next time that I saw Floyd, also in Reno, I again went up to say hello to him, and although very cordial, he seemed to be looking right through me. I thought perhaps he was angry at me for some reason, and it wasn't until I learned a year or so later, that he had Alzheimer's that I fully understood why.

ANOTHER FRIEND, THE LATE manager/promoter Ted Walker of Carson City, used to take me on some of his long car trips to Caldwell and Boise, Idaho, where he was actively promoting fights. We drove using his old station wagon and he would tell stories that would make one wish that they had a tape recorder and 100 or so blank tapes on hand as well. I could have used those stories to fill this entire book. Ted was one of a kind, one of the last of a dying breed.

Woozel, Boxing and Me

In truth, I'm old school and not the least bit enthralled by most of the up and coming fighters in the boxing world today. But because this is boxing, it will survive like it always has, and hopefully someday take its rightful place among the major sports.

I can remember clearly when Bay Area Boxing Hall of Fame founder Sammy Stein and his wife, both in their 60's at the time, came in from the Bay Area, and upon Sammy's request, I took them both to the Carson City gym to meet Ted Walker and have them look around. I pointed to a photo on the wall of a female boxer who used to fight for Ted, asking whatever became of her. Without batting an eye Ted, looked up, "Oh, that lesbian, she's still working in some dildo making factory in Sacramento." It was a bit embarrassing, even for a crusty old guy like me.

But, Ted, for all his outward gruffness had a heart as big as all outdoors. Rest in peace my old friend, we will meet again.

ANOTHER GOOD FRIEND I have in the sport is Moe Smith, a former professional wrestler, who at the time we met, was actively involved in Reno boxing as a promoter, matchmaker, and booking agent. Moe is a great guy, who along with his lovely wife Marcia, now promotes boxing and other events in Couer d'Alene, Idaho, and remains a good friend. In fact, I used Moe as the physical model for a character in my first boxing book, "Off the Canvas."

I recall the fights at the "Cow Pasture" in Gardnerville, Nevada. An event put on by the late Sharkey Begovich, owner of 'Sharkey's Nugget', the local casino in Gardnerville. The casino has been sold, the cow pasture is gone now and sadly the cows that remain no longer have any live entertainment to enjoy.

Sharkey's Casino is also under new ownership, as Sharkey passed away a few years back. Sharkey was in the boxing business for more than 30 years and was a great guy. His real first name was Milos, but he took the nickname "Sharkey" because former heavyweight champion Jack Sharkey was his favorite fighter.

For the record, Sharkey had a large collection of old-time boxing memorabilia that would be the envy of almost every fight fan and memorabilia collector, which was, for the most-part, sold at auction in Reno after his passing.

I remember a boxing card that was put on at the "Cow Pasture" by promoter Moe Smith in which he unintentionally kept his word. Moe had long promised the local fans to bring pro wrestling to Northern Nevada.

Moe strangely kept his promise when the late local fighter, Clinton Reymus and Herman Cavasuela of California, two rival middleweights, decided to "get it on" in any and every way possible. Whenever they fought each other they took no prisoners, and it always brought out the crowd.

At that time they were scheduled for a boxing re-match that quickly turned into a wrestling match, where they rolled out of the ring and continued to pound away at each other near the seated fans. Vince McMahon, if he had seen this event, would have hired Moe, himself a former professional wrestler, to promote matches for him. Reymus - Cavasuela was, to be sure, a great rivalry and fan attraction for many years.

Reymus was a Native American who sadly was beset by alcohol problems. He committed suicide by the railroad tracks in Reno, and a short time later Cavasuela was badly injured in a car accident in California and never fought again, but, thankfully, he has recovered and reportedly is doing very well.

Ted Walker often warned me to stay away from Reymus when he was drinking, as he could become very nasty and dangerous. Strangely, or not, Clint and I had always got along well, even when he was drinking, and used to offer to buy me drinks whenever he saw me. Sometimes, time permitting, I would accept, and would sit down and chat with him a bit.

I REMEMBER SEEING a fight, can't recall if it was on television or at ringside, when after a knockdown and standing eight count, the referee asked the dazed fighter, "Do you know where you are?" The question would be considered legit to see if the fighter had sustained a concussion. The fighter looked at the ref, still apparently dazed, and responded "Yeah, I'm right here! Can't you see that?" The ref couldn't question the logic to that answer or bother to answer that question, so he let the fight continue. Fortunately no one was hurt.

THERE WAS A TIME, not that many years back, when pro-am fight cards (no longer recognized by the Commission) were going strong in Nevada, and on one particular bout card that Ted Walker was promoting, a prelim pro bout fell out at the last minute. Ted would never panic. He simply went back into the dressing room where the amateurs were getting ready and asked the fighters on hand: "Which one of you guys want to turn pro tonight"?

There are a lot of Bruce "Mouse" Strauss stories that are around and the only one that everyone seems to swear to is when he fought twice in one-night on the same card, once as himself and once as his identical twin brother (which he didn't have). It didn't matter, he lost both fights.

I remember the days when there were 15 round championship fights, eight or nine weight divisions and only one legitimate world champion. Life for the writer and the fan was so much easier in those days of the recent past. Today, trying to remember all the different champions and the sanctioning bodies whom they represent is all but impossible, even to someone like myself who has been in (and out) of boxing most of my life.

IN MORE RECENT YEARS, I can recall being at the great Hagler/Hearns three-round, give and take war at Caesars Palace and meeting the late, great Sugar Ray Robinson and his wife Millie. At that time he was suffering from Alzheimers.

The High and the Flighty

I recall seeing and *not* recognizing at first, the then Executive Director of the Nevada Athletic Commission, Chuck Minker, who was in a wheelchair, on oxygen and had wasted away to skin and bones from a very rare form of lung cancer. Chuck had always been a health nut who never even smoked.

Chuck said hello to me, and it took me a minute to figure out who was speaking to me. Chuck was always so active and healthy. Sad. He was a good guy. Fortunately Marc Ratner, a friend of Chuck's (and of boxing) who took over as Executive Director from Minker, did a great job in his place.

I remember sitting, in the press room with legendary referee Mills Lane, watching the Gabe Ruelas/Jimmy Garcia fight at Caesar's Palace, with Mills screaming at referee (via TV) the late Mitch Halpern, to stop the fight .in round ten. He didn't and Garcia was allowed to continue, and he had to be carried from the ring in the final round.

Garcia passed away shortly afterwards. He could have quit and no one would have lost an ounce of respect for him, but the Latino machismo and the urging of his family to continue was what ultimately got him killed. Although, to this day, I believe the fight doctor at ringside was the one who should have stopped the one-sided fight. But hell, I'm not a doctor and he is, and as I understand it, a damn good one (some may argue that I'm not even a writer) and I try to never second guess a professional.

I truly believe that Mitch Halpern was never the same as a result of Garcia's death, and that he committed suicide in Las Vegas not too long afterwards. I had interviewed Chuck a few months earlier, and the depression they said he had been suffering from, sure didn't seem a bit evident to me. He even denied, when I asked, that the ring death was on his conscience. Some of his closest friends also have told me that the Garcia tragedy had nothing to do with Halpern's suicide and had to do solely with problems with his girlfriend.. Again, I'll take their word for it.

Woozel, Boxing and Me

I REMEMBER SITTING at the post fight press conference at the Riviera Hotel in Las Vegas when Larry Holmes made his infamous remark about Rocky Marciano not being able to carry his jock strap.

I was seated between legendary boxing writers Dick Young and Jack Fiske, when both scribes, being old-school, scored the bout for Holmes. (Up until that time it was generally accepted that you had to do enough to take the fight from the champion). We just looked at each other in shock, as Holmes made his angry remarks, not believing what we had just heard Holmes say.

I have known Larry Holmes for some time, and I truly believe that he made that remark out of frustration, having come so close to Rocky's 49-0 record, only to lose a very close decision. Larry is certainly not a racist as some people immediately felt. For the record I also had Michael Spinks, as the winner of the contest, albeit barely.

ALSO, AT THE RIVIERA I recall doing an interview with former heavyweight contender, Earnie Shavers, a good guy. I had invited him to do the interview over breakfast, and at that he meal gave me a very good interview and a restaurant bill of more than $35. That man can eat!

In mid-2005 I was asked to host a benefit to raise money for the opening of the Muhammad Ali Cultural Center, at Ricky's Sports Bar in Oakland, California. Being uncomfortable reading from a prepared script, I decided to wing it, which I have always been best at doing.

I gave a brief talk on why I thought Muhammad Ali was the best heavyweight of all time, and then had to introduce the two guys who do outstanding work in impersonating Ali and Howard Cosell.

I simply said that "before I introduce "The Greatest" allow me to introduce the many who thinks he's the greatest "(Cosell). That opening went fine. But remembering to always be prepared, I had a second line ready if I screwed up the opening: "OK, how would you guys go about introducing a dead man?"

Another story that I've been able to confirm was that many years ago, in Pittsburgh, a fighter named Sammy Secret was carrying a fighter, when he found out that he had to catch a train (change in schedule). He went to his opponent's corner and congratulated him on a good fight. His foe was taken aback. "This fight's not over yet," he said. Secret responded "No, but it soon will be." Sammy scored a quick knockout in the next round.

I GET ASKED OFTEN if I have any regrets in choosing boxing as my sport of choice and boxing journalism as an occupation. The truth is that as of this writing, I haven't made any money at it. But boxing has offered me nothing but great friends and great experiences, two things that money cannot buy, although maybe it can buy great experiences. I have no regrets.

I'd change absolutely nothing in my life, except perhaps to make a few more bucks so my wife and I would be able to enjoy our senior years more than we currently are. Yet, I still remain firm in my belief that you can always have money, it will come and go, but real friends are far more valuable to me, as they are a rare commodity to most people. Besides, in what other profession could I meet so many great folks who are now/were or will probably become far nuttier than myself, and that's saying a lot.

THE FOLLOWING ARE FROM FRED RYAN, long-time friend, and owner and operator of Portland, Oregon's Grand Ave Gym:

- Late into a show on a walk out bout, the timekeeper bellows "second's out" the bell sounds and I back down the steps keeping an eye on the action and plant my foot squarely in a half filled spit bucket. I had presence of

Woozel, Boxing and Me

mind to look around to see if anybody saw this. They didn't seem to . But I had an awful wet and squishy foot and a wet pant leg for the rest of the evening. Awful.

🏆 This from promoter Steve Canton, (by way of Fred Ryan) who had booked a young KO Artist from Nicaragua into a 6 round bout for his USA debut for $200 bucks per round, which was the going rate at the time. After a dull and boring contest which the kid won, Steve asked the youngster why he looked so lackluster as if he was carrying his opponent. I really was just carrying him replied the kid, "I wanted the whole $1200 bucks.

🏆 A Portland, Oregon company had built a prototype boxing robot to be marketed and sold to fighters and trainers as a workout sparring partner. This thing was incredible, about 6 feet tall like a black rubber mannequin with an ugly face in a boxing pose, It could jab, hook and right cross with punches that could be set from flyweight to heavyweight velocity. It seemed a great idea until their corporate attorney saw this thing and told them, "This robot was one big liability." Fred Ryan found out about it and got the robot to set up in the lobby of his boxing event. He than trucked him over to the arena and wheeled him into the coat check room, turned out the light and shut the door. Later in the afternoon, the marketing director had to get something out of there, and when he entered and turned on the light, he got the shock of a lifetime, seeing what was standing in front of him in a boxing pose. He had to go home to change his suit pants.

🏆 Fred fondly recalls: Some things are a mystery and I have never stopped learning but this story is a wonder to me. I was at an Arizona event when an ancient boxer without a handler asked me to wrap him up (his hands) and work his corner and I obliged.

The High and the Flighty

🏆 I can't recall his name. He was an old war horse that was still packing some sap and knew his way around the ring more then just a little bit. Along about the end of the 4th round of a scheduled six, he isn't doing very good and mentions that the guy is giving him fits. I told him that his opponent was a converted southpaw. "He Is? -He Is? How do you know that?" and sits bolt upright on his stool. "I saw him eating in the restaurant and watched him sign his contract this morning," I tell him. He replies, "Oh well, I'll just go out there and fix him next round." With that he leaps off the stool like an unattached boxer. That round wasn't 30 seconds into time when he had his winning opponent stretched for the count. I didn't see the knockout as I had to get back to the dressing room and my next boxer and will always regret that I never got to ask him what method he had used to handle a converted left-handed opponent. I suppose I am still learning.

🏆 On the day of a boxing event I was running low on Vaseline in my kit bag and made it up to the Dollar store and bought a couple jars of grease. I didn't notice it at the time, but in the dressing room I discovered this petroleum jelly was "Baby Scent" and I was stuck. It was a hot night and the opponent was a clincher, so between rounds I was pretty liberal in greasing my fighters sides with this stuff and man did everything start to smell pretty sweet in the late rounds. The ref came over and asked me if I was spraying perfume on my boxer and I told him it might be the other guy's hair oil. He actually went over and sniffed the other guy's hair. The first line of defense is to always deny everything.

🏆 After an event, we were stacking the chairs and taking down the ring and one kid was standing in the back drinking a beer. I asked him how he liked the show and he said he loved it but during the bouts someone had broken into his car in the parking lot and had stolen his stereo. I went upstairs and cornered the building manager and said that kid down there said he had his car broken into outside and I paid you for an outside security guard for the parking lot. The manager took the cigar out of his mouth and said, "That kid *WAS* the outside security guard. He came in to watch the show." Poetic Justice, and he was the only break-in that night.

🏆 GOOD FRIEND AND boxing buff Harrin Platzner tells this true ring story of his father, Herb. "Herb told me once that his first boxing match was held in the Bronx and at the end they gave him a watch when he won. He was very annoyed because he wanted food and couldn't figure out how he was going to eat the watch.

🏆 MARVIS FRAZIER told this one to Pennsylvania Athletic Commissioner Greg Sirb, who kindly passes it along: "Boxing – It's where you get your money took, your brains shook and maybe get your name in the undertaker's book".

🏆 DEREK CALLAHAN gives us some insight as told by former welterweight champ Carlos Ortiz: "I'm a dog lover, and I had a little dog when I was 12 years old. My mother sent me to the store so I decided to take my little dog with me. While I was in the store, the dog got scared from the traffic noise and ran out the door. I ran after him and he ran into the street. A car came – and boom! And it hit him. It killed my little dog and I was devastated. I got the dog onto the sidewalk, all the people were around me, I was crying and crying over the dog. All of a sudden a photographer from the NY Daily News passed by, and took a picture. That picture became picture of the year in that newspaper. It was fantastic! I've got the picture and

I look at it every day. That was the greatest thing to ever happen to me."

FOR THE RECORD former middleweight champion Gene Fullmer and his wife, once ran a mink farm in Utah.***

I WAS FORTUNATE ENOUGH to be in Las Vegas, with wife Lois, when Max Schmeling was being honored at the Sands Hotel. Max had saved two brothers, the Lewin's, from the Nazi's, one grew up to own this Casino. A lot of dignitaries were on hand for this event, which was hosted by my good friend, the late Jack Welsh. Among those on hand included Alexis Arguello, and Mike Tyson, to name a few. At the event, everyone partook in the feast that included the first food and beer flown in from East Germany, since the fall of the Berlin Wall.

Another favorite memory, which goes way back, concerns former heavyweight champion Lennox Lewis, before he became a world champion. I was asked to find a training camp in Northern Nevada for Lennox to train, which I did. Lennox had a room at the old Ormsby House in Carson City, where I ventured (invited of course) to his room for an interview. I found Lewis to be a quite pleasant, but serious sort. When I walked in the room, he was on the bed, playing chess with one of his trainers. Lennox, at least in my novice eyes, seemed to be an outstanding chess player, and when he challenged me to a game, I backed down. No reason to be embarrassed.

SOME MORE BOXING quotes to share:

- "If I refereed a John Ruiz fight, I'd take away a point every round." Said by top referee Frank Cappuccino.

🏆 "I quit school in the sixth grade because of pneumonia. Not because I had it, but because I couldn't spell it." Said by former middleweight great Rocky Graziano.

A TRUE STORY FROM DAVID RUFF "Back in 1997, in Syracuse, N.Y., announcer/writer Larry Tournambe and I were going to the International Boxing Hall of Fame inductions in Canastota NY. We were staying at the Hampton Inn. When I was going into the bathroom to get a shower after Larry had taken his, Larry told me that he had to go down to the lobby to see if they still had the continental breakfast. He forgot to take his door key, and I took a long shower.

The steam of the shower set off the fire alarm. Suddenly, everybody is running around the hotel to see where the fire is. Larry returns to the room and sees the steam that was going under the door, (from the shower). He quickly went downstairs to tell them that I was still in the room; but no one listened to him. He tries to get the key for the room when he sees the Syracuse firemen quickly running up to our floor.

Larry goes back to the front desk and keeps trying to tell them about the key. Finally, after cussing them out, and letting them know that I was disabled, they figure out it was me in the shower causing the steam that had caused the alarm to go off. The Syracuse firemen also finally figured out that it was a false alarm, after seeing me coming out of the shower (no more steam). Aside from that incident, it was a fine trip to the boxing Hall of Fame.

FROM MY MATE JOHN MCDOUGALL, boxing commissioner from New South Wales, Australia:

Probably the funniest thing, to me happened many years ago when we were building the Snowy River Hydro Electric plant in the Australian Alps. It was a big operation and a lot of migrant labor was employed there. A fight night was put on to break the monotony for the workers and was attended by Peter Ustinov, the famed actor, who was in the area with Deborah Kerr and Robert Mitchum making the film, "The Sundowners."

It was an outdoor promotion and one of the bouts was between two tent fighters who were great at putting on a show and had fought each other about 50 times in the past. They would be up and down and staggering about and were great performers and filled out many a fight card. Their names were Mickey Fernandez and Normie Miller.

Australia's best known referee at the time was Ray Mitchell, who had a high opinion of himself and knew and had refereed these two in their bouts many times. As a referee he prided himself on knowing everything, or so he thought.

I was at the promotion, as I happened to be in the area on business, and went along and got involved in the corner. The battle waged along with first one boxer would appearing to be on top and then the other. After one particular round, Fernandez staggered to his corner and collapsed onto the stool, both eyes closed, and for all intents and purposes, almost unconscious. The referee rushed to the corner to ask the corner men if Mickey needed the doctor as he seemed to be in a bad way and he was stopping the fight. With that Fernandez opened one eye and without looking up, said, "Fuck off Ray will you? Your spoiling the fun."

At a function afterwards we gave the referee some schtick getting sucked in as he did, and Ustinov was in hysterics and enjoyed the incident in particular and the whole night in general.

VETERAN HIGHLY RESPECTED boxing writer and friend Danny Wambolt adds the following three stories:

- When Max Baer and Jimmy Braddock, at the time ex-heavyweight champions, were introduced to Francis Cardinal Spellman at an Eagles Convention, they both knelt to kiss his ring. Always fast with his quips, Max said to the Cardinal, "This must be the first time anybody had two heavyweight champions on the floor at the same time."

🏆 In the 1930's, Clem McCarthy, famed radio announcer before the dawn of sports on television, was known for his rapid, fiery delivery. Clem could make the worst fight into an exciting massacre. People at home listening to the radio would hear Clem with his fiery delivery on punches being thrown, sound like a machine gun being fired, even though less than a dozen punches would be thrown in the round. One night in one of Max Baer's fights, he could hear McCarthy announcing his punches that he was hardly throwing. In about round four, he put up his gloved hand to his opponent and said "Hold on a minute." Reaching over the ropes, he looked down at Clem who was at the mike and said, "Will you slow down until I can catch up with you?"

🏆 The night that Max Baer died, he had checked into a hotel after a personal autograph signing appearance and shortly after fell ill. He called the front desk and asked if they had a doctor? The clerk at the desk replied, "We have a house doctor." To which Max replied: "I don't want a house doctor, I want a people doctor."

ROUND IX:
Two chapters written or contributed to, by young and talented scribe Derek Callahan

The Punchline

"In the clearing stands a boxer and a fighter by his trade, and he carries the reminders, of every glove that laid him down or cut him 'til he cried out, in his anger and his shame, 'I am leaving, I am leaving, but the fighter still remains...'"
–Simon & Garfunkel

AS A WRESTLER IN HIGH school I was always trying to improve. Always working, always striving, because that's the only way I was going to be anything besides a pair of glasses atop shoulders that felt the mat dozens of times in a career. I had my motivation, and I had a sense of the game to help me along. I didn't have the natural talent or ambition though, and I realized all this one day some winters ago.

The County wrestling championships were the weekend before, and at practice the Monday after, I dug in to wrestle a teammate. He was one of the upperclassmen who competed well enough over the past weekend to be called "Champ," and I was the freshman who knew my own limits perhaps too

The Punchline

well. I was sure by this time that I had no future as an athlete, certainly not in my chosen sports, the kinds too violent to play. In boxing and wrestling you just *do*.

So squaring off with the new local champ, an obstacle seventy pounds heavier and at least eight thousand times better than myself, this was the first time I went into competition as an observer. I knew I wanted to be a sportswriter, but I had ultimately about a season and a half left in my wrestling career. I was stuck on the tracks, and unfortunately, a two hundred twenty pound train was about to go by. "Hey man," I asked, trying to delay the inevitable, "if I pin you now, does that make me the County champ?" He just shrugged, his intentions of taking me out never really wavering. "I guess so."

Consider me cocky enough to think that I learned a big lesson on my first self-assignment as a sports observer. Right as I was bridging the athlete/observer divide, I became a participatory journalist, a regular outsider. I had all the ingredients: an athlete, minus talent, plus the exact same passion for the sport that any world champ has. That inherent desire to become the champ on a slim, miraculous win must be in all the participatory journalists. The chances of this happening aren't on the level of David slaying Goliath, they're more along the lines of Goliath having heart failure right before the bout could start.

The line of reality is drawn on the mat, and in many cases for pro writers squaring with pro athletes, the boxing ring. At the whistle I shot in at my opponent's legs and got a better grip than I thought I could, kidding myself into thinking that it was my speed, and not his enormous thighs, that allowed me to get a grip. I tried pulling them close to my body as he sprawled back and shook himself clear of my hold. Houses don't have the foundation and balance that this kid had.

About thirty seconds in which he sinewed his left arm through my right pit and jerked it to the side so his hand had a grip on my head like he was palming a groaning basketball, I thought of all the places I'd rather be: a couch, the beach, in a wood-chipper. He flipped me like the other side needed grilling and that was that. I got up though, and was immediately able to give it another go. I had the mentality. Do better; get more attention, live with the perks that come with being the immovable object only seen before in comics and dreams. After practice, I got off the mat a smarter guy. Other jump-in-the-mix writers didn't come out too lucky.

IN *SHADOW BOX* George Plimpton, the king of participatory journalists, described the single most unfortunate amateur to mix it up in the ring with professionals. Albert Payson Terhune was a reporter for the *New York Evening World* when he was assigned to go three rounds with each of the top heavyweights of his day. At first, things were looking up.

"Not only did he know most of the fighters he had been asked to box," writes Plimpton, "but he had already sparred with some of them." He was after all, as Plimpton pointed out, "six foot four and so strong that he was always called on to act as a pallbearer when a member of the *Evening World* staff died."

Gus Ruhlin, Kid McCoy, Tom Sharkey--and here the list gets worse--Jim Corbett, Jim Jeffries, and Bob Fitzsimmons all beat Terhune like they were benefiting from it. Turns out they were. Terhune's editor, in search of as realistic a story as possible, offered a feature in the paper to whoever knocked the unwitting reporter out. The heavyweights were fishing for publicity and Terhune was bait. Nobody could finish the deed, but Terhune walked away with, according to Plimpton, "his left hand broken, two teeth were gone, and his face puffed and stitched."

I cringe when I hear this, but as the cringe fades and my face uncrumples, it starts to feel a lot like a smile. Still, the next time I want to get up at a press conference and yell, "I want Holyfield!" like Chris Farley's Gen. Norm Schwarzkopf on *Saturday Night Live*, I'll think of Terhune. I'll probably shut up too, because as fun as it is to get in the mix, sports are for the fans, and the fans deserve athletes.

The Punchline

BECAUSE OF WHERE most fighters come from, boxing fans don't just get athletes. There's no mainstream collegiate boxing for a reason, and yes, I think it has something to do with the fact that Abercrombie & Fitch doesn't make trunks. For the most part, boxing fans get the type of people who they cross streets to avoid. These are oftentimes the same ones who fight on and learn. Improve. Adapt. This is how a fighter becomes a champion, and how a life less sunny becomes a life less ordinary. Boxing affords people this opportunity. It always has.

Boxing was always tough. When fighters rode rails and dropped by bars to pick up some money and some shots, it was just as severe, maybe more so than modern times. But the first precedent of what it takes to be the shark of the waters was set by John L. Sullivan. When boxing was starting to cook with gas back at the end of the 19th century, a whole lot of pre-Woodstock hippies and machine-era politicians got up to oppose it. But boxing eventually ended up on top because, like its athletes, it is resilient. Like a great fighter, boxing is stoic and boxing wouldn't crumble at the sight of opposition. It was buoyed by pillars, by the excitement of fighters like John L. Sullivan.

When he left Roxbury, Massachusetts to bust down doors of saloons like a muscular version of the Kool-Aid man and scream, as the legend goes, "I can lick any sonofabitch in the house!" he was becoming the first, and most intimidating, advertisement for boxing. Personally I think this type of publicity should continue today with Mike Tyson and a T.G.I. Friday's, but digressing is a dangerous thing to do. So we return.

As the original dominant heavyweight, his record clearly shows that the sport really was taking its first baby steps. While he was indeed the dog of his day, "Sully" in total fought a recorded 26 fighters who were 0-0-0 when they fought him. Obviously all of them went to 0-1-0 afterwards, but these mismatches weren't sporadic. Between October 17th, 1883 and November 10th, 1884, more than a year, Sullivan licked only sonofabitches who had never fought in a ring before. In total, it was 11 straight.

Woozel, Boxing and Me

The "Boston Strong Boy" eventually proved his mettle though when he showed some old fashioned whiskey-in-the-corner stoutness and stopped Jake Kilrain after more than two hours and 75 rounds of fighting. This was the precedent for what it takes: against the tops, you step up. But the men are separated from the boys more publicly when the work is done in front of a big crowd. Even against the not so tops, even in the amateurs, there's a good share of fighters who can't stand to keep on going in the face of adversity. They learn this and move on.

HISTORY HAS RECORDED the winners. After Sullivan there was Jack Johnson, to Jack Dempsey, to Joe Louis, and so on. Even generations get skipped because only so many champs are remembered. The tough fighters who never win a title? Forget it. But over the years there have been fighters and events, insignificant to history, but good reflections upon their trade.

John Hackleman saw his fair share of oddities in the ring. Comfortable living in California after a childhood in Hawaii, it's safe to say that Hackleman, a light heavyweight in the 1980s, is a pretty laid back guy. As an amateur he and his team traveled far to a show and he watched his teammate go to the center of the ring to get stared down by, as Hackleman remembers, "this glitzy guy, wearing rhinestones. This was before *Rocky* but he came out looking like Apollo Creed, real fancy."

Mando Ramos, Hackleman's stablemate, would be the decided underdog in the fight, and that was obvious as they stood in the center of the ring, one doing a stare-down and one doing a literal stare-up. "Mando's looking around like he doesn't know what the hell's going on. He's this Mexican guy that barely speaks English that fixes refrigerators all week in Santa Monica," says Hackleman. Standing in his Converse tennis shoes and wearing PE shorts for boxing trunks, Ramos looked more suited to be walking to a pool than getting into a fight.

The Punchline

"The bell rings, Mando stumbles out, not much footwork and throws a lazy straight right, tags the guy and puts him on his butt," says Hackleman.

"The guy stands up while the referee is still counting, walks through the ropes while the crowd is going nuts. He's leaving the ring with his gloves still on, he walks up the aisle, we're following him, his girlfriend starts running behind him. She opens the door to their car, and they just drive away." Nobody can blame Mando's victim though of not making the count.

The man who fell to the almost accidental right hand of Mando Ramos was more glitz than guts, more diamonds and less hearts. He's Exhibit A of those who get cleared out by the ones who harbor serious motivation. There's more where this behavior came from.

"I fought this short, stocky Mexican guy and it's a tough fight but I'm definitely kicking his ass," begins Hackleman. "He won't come out for the fourth round so the referee stops the fight. I didn't drop him or anything but he stops in the middle of the fight. He's still sitting on his stool so I thought he may have dislocated his shoulder or something crazy. I walk over to his corner, shake his hand. He looks up at me and says: 'Yeah I couldn't go on bro, I had a hair in between my teeth.'" Most of the blame can be put on the corner man of this short, stocky Mexican. Any ring second worth keeping would know to bring floss to the ring. So at the risk of losing all readers who have a sense of humor here: Hackleman won the fight by a hair.

This was a Californian by way of Hawaii who was a magnet for the absurd. Prior to a fight he once paid for his own hotel room out-of-pocket so he didn't have to stay with Ed Cousins, a tetchy old trainer who was a real Sherlock Holmes at finding fault.

"I was training at Muhammad Ali's boxing gym in Santa Monica. The guy was probably 90 then and he would not shut up, he was always ragging on everything," recalls Hackleman. "You could knock a guy out in the first round and, 'Aah that guy was a bum ya shudda knocked him out 10 seconds sooner.'"

Every gym has one. For one of his fights, Hackleman had Cousins work his corner on the recommendation of a stablemate. "I come back after like three rounds. I'm beating the guy but it's a pretty close fight and he's just ragging on me, 'keep ya gahddamn hands up.' After the fourth round I just walked back to the neutral corner. The referee thought I was disoriented he came running over," says Hackleman.

"I go, 'I am not going back into that corner unless he shuts up.' Ed Cousins was just laughing, 'get over here gahddamnit.' I went and knocked the guy out the next round anyway. I was tired of him yelling so much, he was so irritating."

BOXING CAN BECOME so absurd, it's a zaniness that boxers just learn to work through. The good ones work through it because they see no obstacles. As Henry Ford put it, they see none of, "those frightful things you see when you take your eyes off your goal."

The unhinged desire to just do better is lodged within the existence of the best athletes. The deranged will to focus on one thing over the course of a lifetime up until an athlete's final playing days isn't exclusive to boxing. In *The Village Voice* in 1991 Paul Solotaroff summed up a champion's mentality through Steve Michalik, a bodybuilder cut loose from sensibility, a comet whose sole destination would be up, no sacrifice too big to make. Solotaroff powerfully describes Michalik's lesson to a teenager who wanted to be just like his hero. Kids cry when they find out that Barry Bonds won't sign an autograph? They're considered disillusioned? Well they have another think coming.

The young man had to have felt lucky when he got the chance to work with Michalik, who met him at the beach early in the morning to train. To the boy, this was sparring with Tyson, roadwork with Ali. In the water, Solotaroff writes, "Michalik suddenly seized the kid by his scalp and pushed him under a wave...the air bubbles stopped, whereupon he dragged him out by the hood and threw him, gasping, on the beach.

'When you want the title as bad as you wanted that last fucking breath...then and only then can you come talk to me.'" It can be assumed that the boy didn't return any time soon. But who knows?

There are the outrageous ones in every walk of life. The list is long of the Steve Michalik's of the world who have the intensity to bring down ceilings regardless of who is under them. These are the Bazooka's versus the Palooka's that Hackleman remembers with laughter. Not all fighters shine more from their rhinestones than from their talent, and not all of them get frustrated by that thing in their teeth that no matter how hard they try, they can't guide out with their tongue. Every fighter will run into a Bazooka if he fights long enough. Vinnie Curto ran into a few, but when he did, things clicked because he was one too.

Curto was once managed by Sylvester Stallone. He and other fighters would help with security around Sly's mansion, and in turn, get to live in the type of style that few fighters revel in. For a guy like Curto who paid his dues in squalor, life in a mansion was about as foreign as life on Pluto, only the mansion was bigger. When he moved in, culture shock was in order; so much so that he rejected the luxury and moved in with Hackleman.

"I lived in this little ghetto, a room basically, in Venice, California," remembers Hackleman. "He lived in Sylvester Stallone's mansion. Why would he stay in my little ghetto when he could stay there?" So Hackleman asked. In so many words, Vinnie responded: "Aah there's too much glitz over there, I gotta be back in the ghetto so I could feel like I'm a fighter again." It worked, too. Vinnie Curto went on to fight until 1996, holding a cruiserweight alphabet title in the process.

Part of the continual improvement of a fighter is that he gets to know himself. Curto knew that a life of luxury would only soften him up for the hammers. A great guy once said,

"You can either be the hammer or the nail," and in a mansion, Curto was becoming the nail. He learned his lesson his own way. Others learn their lessons early on and in the ring.

Light heavyweight Billy Wagner was on his way up when he fought Art Miller. Wagner was younger, more fit, more energetic and ready to make Miller a stepping stone. They called him "Curley" Miller because he didn't have a hair on his head. His brother Larry wanted to know if the tires on Curley's bicycle had any air left in them. Miller didn't look like his legs were what they used to be; he certainly wasn't going to be a runner. Billy remembers Larry telling him, "'Don't worry about this Curley Miller guy, his legs are shot.'" At the weigh-in, the difference between the two was stark. "I thought, this is embarrassing, I am fighting an old man," says Wagner. "After 15 seconds of the first round of this fight with a so-called old man, he hit me with a left hook and broke my nose flat over, he just caught the bridge of my nose. After a couple of rounds, I couldn't breathe; my cheap double mouthpiece kept falling out." He wasn't a runner anymore that was obvious. In what was to be the fourth yet toughest fight of Wagner's career, he dug in and eventually got the win. "Afterwards," remembers Wagner. "I said, 'Larry he didn't kick me once but his arms are working.'"

DO BETTER. TRY HARDER. PRESS ON. Learn more and push back when pushed. I learned it on the wrestling mats, Vinnie Curto learned it in the ghetto that he couldn't help but retain, and Billy Wagner learned it in the ring with a busted nose. John L. Sully probably learned it when he vowed not to lose to Kilrain so many decades ago. But nobody learns these things alone, least of all fighters. That's because part of boxing is about relationships--the relationship between two fighters before, during and after a fight, but also relationships that Edison on his best day couldn't invent.

Some of the most influential people swoop in, sweep a fighter off his feet like he's a potential prom date, and make as

The Punchline

much money off of him as possible. Pow! Bam! and a deal is made. Sometimes the promoter/fighter relationship is positive, sometimes it's not. At least once, it's funny. Better yet, how it came about is funny.

The prevailing thought is that Don King went down to Foreman/Frazier I with Smokin' Joe and left with Big George. But that's not the way everyone saw it happening.

Roy Foreman was just a kid supporting his big brother. If Big George played soccer, Roy would be at the soccer field. If George liked hockey, Roy would buy a sweater and get out to the ice because that's the kind of family that the Foreman's were. But the case was that George was on his way to Jamaica to get into a fight. Records point to four different George Foremans that competed in the ring. Three of them have a combined record of 1-12. The other is the real George Foreman, the one who took his little brother to Jamaica in 1973 to watch a fight. For a young guy like Roy, playing hookey to traipse around Jamaica was as good as it got. One day, after watching his big brother work out, Roy left and was walking down the street. He was approached by a stranger. "Hey man, I'm Donald Ray King," said the stranger. "What's your name?" Thinking little of meeting this unknown fan, who had seen at the workout that Roy was in the Foreman family, Roy answered back: "Roy Dean." "Man we got the same initials!" exclaimed Don. Decades later, Roy looked back on the meeting. "This is the first way he starts playin' his mind game," said Roy. The two new friends, one continuously excited and one perplexed, walked along. This was fight time in Kingston, and there was no telling who would bump into whom. Roy Dean and Donald Ray bumped into a singer.

"Pearl Bailey!" shouted Don when he saw the star. "How you doing Pearl!?" Roy, still looking back on the occasion, reminisced. "I thought he knew Pearl Bailey, it was the first time in his life meeting her. Of course he had to make a nuisance of himself." Back in Kingston, Don introduced Pearl to Roy. "This is Roy Foreman, this is my little brother," said Don.

Thirty-two years later, Roy grinned, "Now I'm his little brother all of a sudden. Boy he set me up all the way," he laughed.

Fight time rolled around and George stamped himself a place on the boxing map. It was *The Ring* magazine's fight of the year for 1973, but it didn't even last two rounds. Joe Frazier was decked three times in the first and three in the second. Foreman scored a double hat trick, and celebrated in his locker room after the fight.

"We're back in the dressing room with the Jamaican police," says Roy. "I look up at the door and here's Don King and they got him pinned up. They're getting ready to beat him across the head with those clubs." Don looked up to Roy, and as the younger Foreman remembers it, yells, "Hey man tell him we're family, I'm a brother man! Tell him! That's my brother!" Buddy-buddy with them from before the fight, Roy waved the Jamaican police off of Don King.

"That's how he got next to George, how he got George to sign the contract for Africa. I don't know if that's one of the best things ever or one of the worst things ever," says Roy. "Of course Don will never tell that because it sounds better the other way for him but that's how it happened. Six or seven months later he was getting George to sign the contract for George and Ali to fight in Africa." Don and Roy are good friends to this day. One's still excited, and the other, not so perplexed anymore.

But not all advisors to a boxer have to finagle an angle and jimmy their way into a fighter's life like they're picking a lock. Trainers especially forge a bond with their fighter and instill in him the idea that no good will come unless he knows that that journey, the one that begins with a single step, is a damn hard one. It can't be made without fighting and without getting fired up. No matter what.

Many brawl for the want of the fame, money, glory and the ubiquitous prospect of buying mom a house. Others fight for mom because she can't see her son perform any more. It isn't uncommon: Oscar de la Hoya felt the presence of his late mother when he won his gold at the Barcelona Olympics.

The Punchline

Sixteen years earlier, Howard Davis Jr. had a similar sensation. His mom passed on three days before he was set to fight in the 1976 Montreal Games, and the tragedy made him quit. It didn't make his coach quit on him though.

While Pat Nappi, the other coach, was talking to Davis's father on the phone, Coach Tom "Sarge" Johnson put his hand on the young fighter's shoulder and asked, "Son, are you sure you want to go home? What would your mother think?"

Davis snatched the phone from Nappi. "Dad, I am doing this for mom," he said to his father. Years later, Davis recounts, "My mother's last words to me were, "Good luck and you better bring home that gold." With that in mind, Davis had one choice: go out, and bring that gold on home.

"My father started crying on the phone. I actually got mad at my father for crying," says Davis. "To me at the time, it was a sign of weakness. At that time I felt strong. It was almost like an epiphany. It really was an epiphany. Something really came over me. I knew what my mission was." Davis eventually got the gold at 132 pounds and won the Val Barker award, denoting him the Outstanding Boxer of the Games. He maintains to this day that as an amateur, the easiest fights he had were the ones in the Olympics. It was domination fueled by emotion, and his mom did that for him. Fortunately, most fighters don't have to endure tragedy to do their best. Their spark comes from the old man who gets in, and stays in their faces between rounds.

THE BEST TRAINERS save their words and advise through actions. When they talk, they say something. The best trainers are educators. Their classrooms are gyms, their chalkboards boxing rings. They know a challenge. They don't rely on, as trainer Jesse Reid puts it the, "straight A student," to fuel their stable. Sometimes, they'll have to put a guy in time out.

Thell Torrence, a trainer who was once a student of Eddie Futch, recalls one such time. "He did not like guys talking to his fighters when they're training," says Torrence of Futch.

"We was at the ring one day, and I was boxing somebody, and a guy kept talking, and he asked him to be quiet, 'don't talk to my fighter.'" They walked over to the speed bag where all their workouts would end. "Guy says, 'come back with a right hand!' Eddie says, 'excuse me. Don't talk to my fighter, I'm training my fighter.' Next time he's doing it again, 'come back with a left hook!' Eddie walked over," continues Torrence. The middle-aged Futch approached the backseat driver, a man well over six feet. "Didn't I tell you not to talk to my fighter?" Torrence remembers Eddie asking. The driver inquired as to what Futch might consider doing about it.

"When you hit a guy and he reaches for you, you step around and keep turning and turning," explains Torrence. "This guy went to reach at Eddie. When the guy went to grab him, he just pivoted off, threw a left hook, pivot again, another left hook, another left hook and the guy fell flat on his face. Aah, it was something. We grabbed the guy, picked him up and threw him out of the gym."

As remembered by Torrence, Eddie took a deep breath over his work and wondered aloud. "You go look for a fight, why would you go in a place where there's nothing but fighters? How smart do you have to be?"

The guy that Futch took out had a chip on his shoulder, but even he would be given the chance to reform under Jesse Reid. Having trained nearly 20 world champions, Reid knows the thug life that boxers try, and many times fail, to escape. He's knocked out fighters who have pulled guns on him in training and he's had to baby sit world champs who would go off, beat women, commit other crimes, and make themselves a general nuisance to all involved parties. "They couldn't read or write, they can't get a job, why not fight?" asks Reid. "To me, when a coach is a coach, he doesn't just train people just to be world champions, he trains people to be better citizens, and better people, and helps them to make more money than maybe they wouldn't have the same chance to make.

"Stories like that are really what boxing's all about, it's what life's all about. Taking a chance on somebody once in a while,

The Punchline

not because they're the straight A student, or the kid that's the easy guy to train."

Reid's a gambler when it comes to helping out kids who need some direction. It can be gut wrenching to see a boy become a man only to fall back into boyhood when his money and skill dries up. What can be worse, is when that happens to a good guy, a moral fighter who learns the hard way.

This goes back to Thell and Eddie. Torrence remembers losing his first fight. Before the bout his locker room was a circus of hangers-on all looking to get a piece. He was Thell, Inc., and he had a whole lot of emotional investors. After the fight, "I'm sitting in there with my head down, slowly taking my things off, I'm upset that I lost, and there was nobody there but [Eddie] and I," remembers Torrence.

"He walked over to the door, and he threw the door open. He said, 'let them in.' I looked up, now nobody's there but us. I looked up, looked around, and I didn't see nobody so I dropped my head again. He said again, 'let 'em in!' I looked around, I said, 'Eddie. There's nobody here.'" "That's right," he responded. "Your friends are with you right now. Don't ever forget that."

AND ON NOTING the late, great composer of champions Eddie Futch, some advice--good advice, too. "Trust me: don't ever tell a boxing person that they're crazy. All you'll get is a smile and an, 'of course I'm crazy I'm in the boxing business.'" That's just the way it is: crazy people in a business less traveled. They're crazy like the overmatched kid gunning for the toughest opponent for no other reason than because that's how an athlete should be.

Boxers are funny. Many are brutally determined, and the ones who are not are not boxers long. They know how small the difference between success and failure is, and they know that their own definitions of success are all that matters. They know that, years ago, a precedent of toughness was set, and that people are finding out if they can match it in their own worlds. They do it on wrestling mats, in boxing rings. Life is learned through sport.

Boxers can laugh at the absurdity of the lives that they lead, but they know that Eddie Futch had a point when he drove lessons into his fighters when they were most vulnerable. Futch knew, as Reid knows, that to be always searching for better, always learning, always improving and always having the courage to love what you do and who you do it with will make a guy laugh in the face of hard times. It really will, because it's the best thing in the world.

Round X

More from Callahan and Peter Palmiere

A KILLER AND A KITTY CAT: When he came up with all the characters of his stories, Damon Runyon was probably sitting in Lindy's restaurant one idle evening, maybe seeing which young Judy passing by was by no means bad looking. His characters literally sat all around him because Lindy's was the place for Broadway and for all the characters that had to be there to pass by Damon in the first place. The Guys and Dolls that Runyon caroused with were absurd more than somewhat; in his stories Runyon would have thieves delivering babies, gamblers compelling the handicapped to walk, and even killers making friends with kitty cats.

Had these characters been given a chance to put their own two cents into the piggy bank, they might say something like, "What with living in a town like Broadway, we have become practically as absurd as our surroundings, and even though we may have to take someone to town on account of welshing or foul play in a legitimate or otherwise more devious trade, it is just the same as wheat in a bin that we mean no more harm than a man may want to endow upon his ever-loving wife."

Harmless characters, gentle to everyone except those that they wish to cause harm: that's outlandish. That's how I read Runyon, and that's why I'm convinced that two boxers in particular would have struck an awful resonant chord with a writer so keen on absurdity. One might be the most written about man in history; he is much more than comedy.

He has been written about in so much detail, but Muhammad Ali as an amateur seems to be an overlooked character relative to how much he's been looked at as a man. In Ali's case, Zaire and Manila weren't built in a day. Pete and Nick Spanakos were both teammates of his in the late-50s as amateurs, with Nick even joining Ali as a teammate on the Olympic team in 1960. Ali, Cassius Clay still, was just about the same as a teenager as he was as an adult.

"Every team we went to he wasn't disliked, he was hated," remembers Pete. Once when on an amateur team, everyone voted for who the captain would be: Ali got one vote, from himself. And it was no wonder. Before the world knew him as a smack-talking king, he would practice it *anywhere.*

Standing at some bathroom urinals, Pete was between him and Jimmy Otis, another boxer that Ali was set to fight. Pete remembers Ali balking, "You tell Otis over here that I'm gonna whoop his ass, tell him how *bad* I am." While standing at some urinals could really break a guy's concentration, that would not be a deterrent--Ali was always practicing his trash talk. People wonder how he got to be so quick and keen at it; that's probably how.

This was a teenage Ali, who was already baffling his normal friends. This was an Ali who would set himself up for embarrassment, like when he waited all day for Sugar Ray Robinson to come by the bar that he owned so Ali could introduce himself. He tried, and Pete recalls a dejected Ali surprised, wondering, "Do you know he doesn't even know who I am?"

Nick Spanakos remembers a similar Ali, one that wasn't at all different from the one of his athletic prime. "I give him credit. Back in '59 he was telling us that he was gonna make a spot on the 1960 Olympic team, and that he was gonna be a gold medal winner, and that he was gonna be heavyweight champion of the world," says Nick. "Here was a 16, 17-year-old kid realizing his dream."

After that dream was realized in the 1960s Ali was where he was most comfortable, right in the spotlight and causing trouble. He visited classes that his old buddy Nick Spanakos was teaching, as Spanakos was a college professor. "When he came into the school no learning went on whatsoever," says Spanakos. Once while speaking to the class, Ali made a point to the African-American kids that they didn't have a language like other groups of people. To prove his point he said a phrase in Swahili that he memorized.

"A black man got up and said something back in Swahili," says Nick. "Cassius looks at me like, 'what's going on?' I said that's the Swahili teacher." Ali just forgot where he was. He ran into trouble with these intellectuals on more than one occasion.

"When I had him in front of my students, he was telling them how important Islam was to him. One of my black students got up and asked him, 'What's more important to you, your race or your religion?' Ali responded, "Of course my religion." The student had a follow-up: 'Would you marry a white Muslim?' Ali had no answer, but it didn't matter. His charisma took him anywhere he wanted to go."

"He came into the school and the girls in my class rushed him and were putting their phone numbers in his pocket," says Nick, who wondered how Ali got all this attention in one day when it took him all year to get nothing of the sort.

There were so many sides of this Champ; Runyon would have loved to have met him on Broadway, in his town. Ali was a thief who could deliver a baby--so many sides, so many laughs. The task of filling in for Ali in his post-retirement years fell on boxers everywhere. With the limelight having no one star to shine on, it was up to a new class of stars to fill his void. Sugar Ray Leonard came close, and his battles with Thomas Hearns and Marvin Hagler helped, but under the radar during the reign of these three came a different type of absurd. Under the radar came a mind that could be creative, sinister, dedicated, and hysterical. His mind was and is all these things--his body was Macho.

HECTOR CAMACHO WAS famous in the post-Ali years because he wasn't trying to be the next Muhammad Ali; he was trying to be the first Hector Camacho. Runyon never saw someone like this: nobody had. Nobody knew this new breed of star, like his English teacher and advisor, Pat Flannery.

"Heart of gold, anything he had in his life he'd break in two and share," says Flannery on his old student. "I'm not saying a bad word about him because he's a ton of fun." Maybe a bad word could be said about Camacho, depending on what side you're coming from. For Flannery though, it was all a big unpredictable ride being around the type of athletic entertainer that Camacho was. Before he fought Vinny Pazienza (who later legally shortened his last name to Paz) in 1990, he got him a gift at the press conference, a tampon, and he gave it to Pazienza in front of reporters and TV cameras. The gift sat on the podium at the press conference.

"The guy who was in charge of it, very nice fellow who worked for Donald Trump, he said to me, 'Patrick, remove that,' and I was so embarrassed to remove it," remembers Flannery. "I turned red, reached out over the podium and pulled it back out." The stunt followed a tussle Pazienza and Camacho had prior to the press conference at the Plaza Hotel. They were angry at each other at the time, but they knew how to hype up a fight.

"He does not start it, it's always when the other guy starts it," assures Flannery. It's like the time Camacho was definitely not just trying to hype a fight, because the bout was minutes away when it happened. Kato Ali was his 0-6 stepping stone and, as Flannery remembers, "It was a fight where they came to the center of the ring. Kato Ali was making some very dastardly comments and he insulted Camacho once too much and Camacho hauled off and belted him right before the fight started." The man had less than a minute to go before he could hit him for real, but he didn't care "Not a punch, but a slap. Ali's head went back and I'll never forget this," continues Flannery. "Sugar Ray Leonard's mouth opened like the Holland tunnel when he saw it; he had never seen anything like it."

When he's bickering with Vinny then-Pazienza, it looks like he's just trying to hype a fight. When he's slapping guys around directly before he's set to punch them, it looks like he's just trying to get attention. But that's not the case. Camacho has the inherent ability to entertain and keep people on their toes, whether they are fans or friends.

Pat Flannery remembers the night in 1989 before Camacho was to fight Ray Mancini. Camacho had a tradition, but Mancini was going to be a tough fight--it was, with Camacho winning a split decision--and Flannery wanted Camacho to break his habit and just rest the night before the fight. But as with most champions, Camacho was stubborn. He always went dancing the night before bouts, and this was no different.

"I knew this was going to happen, so I hid his clothing. I took my bed and put his dungarees and his shirt, underwear, underneath my mattress," says Flannery. Camacho asked where his clothes went, and Flannery replied, "I sent it out to the cleaners to have everything cleaned so when the fight is over we can make a clean getaway." Not intending the pun, Flannery also probably didn't intend to see this argument keep going. Camacho bickered some more about how he always went dancing before he fought, and this time should be no different. Like a parent refusing his child another hour of baseball in the backyard, Flannery persisted. "You should be resting," he says. Camacho wouldn't have it. "I gotta dance," he replies.

What happened next seems to sum up Camacho in his prime. He got what he wanted, because he was eccentric enough not to care how he got it. This is how Damon Runyon's characters were, and it suggests that a man like Camacho would fit right in with the old dogs of a Broadway gone but not forgotten. "He opens up the door," remembers Flannery. "Walks down the hallway totally nude, presses the elevator button. He won, I panicked." Camacho got his clothes, danced and then he won. Flannery and other handlers don't get enough credit for the troubles they go through to keep their fighters on the straight and narrow, but for every handler trying to keep a fighter calm, there's too many more from an entourage pulling in a different direction. Take Hector Camacho's most faithful friend and supporter, Raymond Muhammad.

Muhammad was bound to a wheelchair after a bullet in his back made sure that he wouldn't walk again. But, he wanted to make it known that handicapped people could do most of the things able-bodied people could do, and even some things that they couldn't. In the span of two weeks he decided to do an impromptu publicity drive for seemingly nothing too specific.

For the first part, he strapped himself to his wheelchair and with a chain, tied one end to the wheelchair, and another end to none other than the *Triboro Bridge*. Yes, he jumped, and yes, he hanged from the bridge spinning and spinning for an entire hour. TV news channels carried the footage of the stunt as police tried to get him back on the bridge.

"It was one of the nuttiest stunts ever pulled," remarks Flannery. As if closing down the bridge wasn't enough, shortly thereafter he closed down the Staten Island ferry when he jumped off. "This guy has useless legs, nothing," reminds Flannery. So naturally, he figured jumping off and coming two puffs from drowning was the thing to do. So within two weeks he closed down the *Triboro* and the ferry. Flannery was able to take it in stride, because Camacho was able to deal with the influences of his friends.

When a group from his entourage was caught by security in a hotel while moving a sofa outside, Flannery recalls Camacho assuring hotel security that, "I don't know anything about those bums." The Champ was careful not to be taken advantage of too much. As Camacho grew older, he calmed down. The transformation to classic role model could never be completed because eccentricity isn't something a person can just take and leave as he pleases. But he got better.

After a party at Pat Flannery's apartment Camacho was on his way down and out when he spotted a pair of keys left in an apartment door. Nobody was near the keys but Camacho and his friends, so up to Flannery's they went. Camacho rang the bell. "What happened you forget something?" asks Pat. Camacho shook his head. "No I want you to witness this though. On the fifth floor a woman left her keys in her door. People will know we were here and they'll think we broke in." So Flannery went with Camacho down a floor and the whole thing went off without a hitch. But Camacho had been through this sort of thing before. "See how we've changed?" he asked expectantly.

"Ordinarily," Flannery said, years ago, they would have walked right in and taken some furniture."

None of this could be very funny if it weren't for Camacho's ridiculous talent. Even though the fights came late in all of their respective careers, Camacho is the only man to twice beat Roberto Duran and knock out "Sugar" Ray Leonard. He's never been knocked out even well into his forties, and holds wins over Howard Davis, Jr., Greg Haugen, and Ray Mancini. The list of great victories and great battles in defeat stand in stark contrast to the reckless yet generous personality that he has. Like Muhammad Ali and all the other characters, to be Runyon, there has to be more to you than people know about.

ALI AND CAMACHO and all other like parties in boxing make it a fun sport with their goofiness. It takes a very affecting sense of laughs to find the depths of boxing funny, and Runyon knew it. He would eat these characters up faster than any meal at Lindy's, and he would know that they were all

Broadway; guts behind the how, and a show to make the guts easier to take.

Take Marty Heller, my grandpa, but more importantly an entertainment lawyer and the inspiration for *The Raging Bull*. Marty once saw something that made him think. In a letter to me he remembers a fight he saw decades in the past featuring an old middleweight champ from the golden era of middleweights:

"These fighters were toward the end of the second round, and this one fighter was getting killed; he was a bloody mess. His manager wanted to stop the fight as his fighter was taking an awful beating. The fighter implored the manager not to stop the fight. 'I can beat him,' he says through a bloody mouth. In the next round the slaughter continued when [the] fighter takes a wild swing, connects on the guy's head and flattens him for the count. He rushes back to his manager saying, 'I told you I can beat him: didn't I tell you?' Now he continues, 'I want Graziano. If I haven't told you a hundred times, I want Graziano!' The manager looks at him saying, 'and I told you a *thousand* times: you are Graziano!'"

That's a crazy yarn that would knit an even crazier sweater. That's boxing. Reflected in it is the humor of Ali, Camacho, so many others. If I've seen it a hundred, if I've seen it a thousand times, I can tell what it is; just a killer and a kitty cat.

Big-Ups

"From the moment I picked your book up until I laid it down, I was convulsed with laughter. Someday I intend reading it."
                                                        Groucho Marx

IF YOU READ NOTHING else of my work, read these tributes so you can see exactly who and what is responsible for the work that you didn't read. Sometimes while being locked into the ungodly hours of the night writing on a pad under covers or typing to the rhythm of the throb in my exhausted head (and I didn't even write a whole book), I would start to convince myself that writing is a solitary process. I was lying.

Without the help of these people, I would be right where I am today - sitting in a leather chair--only with a lot less experience and fun in my life. Professionally, they have been generous and have taught me that it doesn't matter where you start, but where you're going. They have shown me exactly how to treat a fledgling anything: Kipp Kollar and the entire NAGA crew, grappling wizard Dave Ginsberg, Joel Gold and Tom DeFazio of *Full Contact Fighter* magazine, the Boxing Writer's Association of America. Invaluable has been the guidance of Jay Glazer, a football know-it-all who actually knows it all. Thanks and respect is due for Stephen Quadros, Greg Kalikas of Pro Karate Weekly radio, and Sam Sheridan, my editor even though he didn't know he was (I'm sneaky like that).

THE .COM ARMY THAT makes up the good old-fashioned world of digital fight news would be dead without Mike DiSanto and Ron Merrill of *InsideFighting*, Larry Goldberg of *BoxingInsider*, Jeff Sherwood of *Sherdog*, Brad Berkwitt of *RingsideReport*, and Kirik Jenness of *MMA TV*, my second editor and one of the most well-respected men I know.

By the way, *"Outside of a dog, a book is man's best friend. Inside of a dog, it's too dark to read."* -Groucho Marx

Distractions during writing are not always welcome, but when they are coming from Joe Mac, Iceberg, or anything else from South Beach Modeling and Entertainment, I say bring it on...Carroll Wojtyla, relative to Pope John Paul II, taught me not to reject depravity, but to pick and choose what kinds were right for me...Keith MacDougal knows a lot about coaching wrestling, but he knows a helluva lot more about turning boys into men, which he did for me...Jeff Edwards has my ongoing thanks for his skill in acquiring nightclub wristbands, so long as it's continued to be put to good use...Laser Park of West Windsor is the best place in the world for laser tag and kid's birthdays, but an even better place for working with teenage girls...Brian Maynard Welsh wants $100,000 and I say 100,000 of us should give him a buck because he damn well deserves it, but only if he tells me where his energy comes from...Kyle Maynard (no relation) should also tell us common folk where he gets his energy from—wait—he did in his book *No Excuses*, buy it...

The entire 1994 NY Rangers and 1996 NY Yankees are all invited to my next birthday party; guys seriously call me I'll give you the address...Quentin Tarantino did pretty much the same thing Carroll did for me, just with more movie violence mixed with art...Romeo's Restaurant in Plainsboro, New Jersey has the best vodka rigatoni, I suggest you go there now and get some...Frank Sinatra, I'll bet you were a good guy, thanks for 'I Get a Kick out of You' and 'The Way You Look Tonight'…WWPHSS '05 had an all-in-all good time, so I say 'good times,'…Cheers to Will Ferrell and Adam Sandler, architects of my sense of humor and the funniest men in the world, but they had better watch out for my main man Dane Cook…Hugh Hefner, you are my hero for several reasons…To Marvel Comics creator Stan Lee, you have a great choice in grandmas, I will give you that…

Shane Schoepfer has been my right hand for a couple years and wondering how someone can be so lazy yet such a hard worker will literally make ones head explode.

To Mr. and Mrs. Casey Palowich of Plainsboro, this is where I thank you two for trying to bring me down before I even got started. With your actions you've taught me something valuable: no matter how smart you think you are, sometimes you're just dead wrong…Anyone else who has had some negative words or tried to hold me back, thanks because you're half my motivation, sharing that distinction probably with girls…yeah I'd say girls…

The fighters that put in the work and fight the rounds for reasons of their own have my utmost respect…thank you so much to those that told me stories relayed in these chapters, you guys are the reason the sport lives on, which isn't to say that these chapters make the sport live on, but you guys do…Be it with love, laughs or anything else, each member of my family, both extended and immediate, have been a great help in their own way…Grandpa Marty Heller gave me the genes to complete the outfit: you can be a raging bull or sitting duck, but a little of each is probably best…

If you were forgotten, well then chances are you probably should be so cry me a river…But really I've been running back and forth to my computer adding those I've forgotten to this here menagerie of gratitude, and I know I've probably omitted some of the most important people. If you think you should have been included, chances are it's my fault, and I'll feel immediately guilty when you confront me. I'll probably buy you dinner so give it a shot…

Big-Ups

If you've made it this far to the end of the 'Big-Ups' section, you're eligible for either a free backrub from me, or a free small bucket of balls at your nearest driving range next time we meet. To prove you read it all though I'm going to need a verbal list of all the people recognized...Now let's get to the real good stuff shall we?***

WEST COAST BOXING scribe Peter Palmiere, adds these personal insights.

DON KING: 1) At the Lewis-Holyfield Los Angeles rematch press conference: I interviewed Don about the bad decision in the first fight. He said "For all who felt the decision was wrong, turn down the sound of the HBO commentators, look at the fight, then score it" implying viewers were influenced by them.

I said "Don, I did that and still scored the fight 9-3 for Lewis". He gave an unpleasant blank stare and said "That is your opinion and a very valid one, but Colin Hart scored a draw, the head of HBO said it was a draw. The reason for the controversy is me. They say look at the crazy black man with the wild hair."

When I asked how Don explains that all of his critics are black, white and all sort of colors, he said "They do have diversity".

There were many journalists waiting to talk to Don but when some heard my last question to him "What's your favorite chapter in the Bible?" One prominent LA journalist said "Did you hear that shit? That **does it, I'm leaving**".

Lennox Lewis sarcastically said "I didn't know that Don was a Christian".

2) The final Trinidad-De La Hoya Las Vegas presser: I asked King about Bob Arum saying he would fire anyone on his staff if they bet on boxing, King said "That's lonesome Bob. I'm not getting in a morals battle with Lonesome Bob. All I did was

offer a million dollar bet with him and the winner collects the million. There's nothing wrong with that".

When I told him I thought De La Hoya would win. King said "That's a valid opinion. Maybe you should bet a million of your own!" During King's very long speech, De La Hoya looked bored and when our eyes locked, I raised my hand and did a fingers meet the thumb motion regarding his speech and Oscar laughed.

3) The Wright-Mosley I post fight presser: D.K. was there and I asked about his promoting Andrew Golota's comeback fight. I told him that would be a hard sell. He asked me why? "Look at his record for being crazy". King replied "What do you mean"?

I said "Look, he bites people in the ring, he quit in the Tyson and Grant fights and what about his getting arrested for impersonating a cop?" He replied "You're not very forgiving". I responded "Not at $49.95".

Bernard Hopkins: 1) The World Boxing Hall of fame held a press conference announcing Hopkins as their 2001 Fighter of the year for beating Tito Trinidad. Sportswriter Robert Morales was the pr guy for the WBHF and announced that I would do the first interview. Doug Fischer of 'Maxboxing.com' ran up to Morales and said "Do you know what you just did?" Morales replied "What's wrong?" and Fischer replied" You just made Peter Palmiere, who does the longest interviews in boxing; go first with Bernard Hopkins who gives the longest answers!"

Morales said "Oh my god, what did I do?" After about 4 questions, (more than fair considering), the interview ended. Shortly after, Steve Kim of 'Maxboxing.com' wrote a piece called The Peter Principal in which he says "Peter Palmiere is a great guy and an asset to 'Maxboxing' but can never be first in line for an interview. His interviews are longer than Don King's undercards".

Sportscaster Rich Marotta in hearing some of these stories was laughing and called me 'a legend'.

2) Hopkins Interview 2004: I asked Hopkins what the biggest misconception people have about him. He said "I talk too

much". I said "Really? People say I ask too many questions. I guess we have something in common" Hopkins said "You're right!"

3) At the Taylor/Hopkins II post fight presser, The final question was posed by me: I asked Bernard this: "Givin' the mood you're in and the emotions you feel right now, are you open to a third fight with Taylor? Bernard replied "What mood am I in Peter? I don't know what mood you think I am. Want to know what mood I'm in? I'm mad as hell! If you say the wrong thing and you definitely will see what mood I'm in."

4). At a Recent Bob Arum interview: I told Bob that De La Hoya was clearly not interested in a fight with Miguel Cotto or Antonio Margarito, I asked Bob if DLH was that expressive with him. Arum said "he was very expressive", I told him that I thought (DLH) should fight Margarito and he told me to go F myself".

FERNANDO VARGAS & OSCAR DE LA Hoya: The Vargas-De La Hoya pressers: In LA, Vargas said on the podium "I'm a true Mexican. Want to know why? This Mexican has balls" He said that in response to Oscar's trainer, Floyd Mayweather Sr. statement: "Now Oscar was nice to give you advice on the Trinidad fight. Instead you turned your head like Mr. Ed and wound up damn near dead!"

Vargas in an one on one interview with me said "As a fighter, he (Oscar) has no balls. He can't knock me out. He has no power, he has no ass. You have to have an ass to knock me out." De La Hoya when asked about Vargas saying he has no balls said "Well, this is not an x-rated fight so he won't see any of those little private parts." (LITTLE?!?) I asked him at the final conference "Vargas said to knock him out you have to have an ass and you don't have an ass. What's your response?" Oscar said "Tell him to stop looking at my ass!"

Vargas and Nauseous: Vargas started a clothing line called nautilus. I asked him why he called it that and he said "Because it will make you sick". I said "I have a poem for your company.

'Nausiuos is so cool, it will make the women drool". People went in hysterics and Vargas said to me "You're fired!"

MORE FERNANDO VARGAS: Interviewing Vargas at of all places an Oscar De La Hoya Golden Boy Promotions card in LA, Vargas said "I have to fight again because I'm surrounded by all my fans look at all these beautiful brown faces". I said I had a beautiful face too which drew laughs. Vargas said in turn "No, you just have a face!

JULIO CESAR CHAVEZ: Chavez was in town promoting the Jesus Chavez-Floyd Mayweather Jr. Fight and he was drunk. When Fiona Manning, with 'Maxboxng.com' at the time, was interviewing him, he tried to kiss her and stick his tongue in her mouth. Roger Mayweather gently pulled the drunken great away and Chavez (with words slurring) said "Roger, I like women!"

Later when I was interviewing him, he took exception to a question I asked and bit me on the stomach. I continued the interview without flinching and all of this is on video. And there was no blood and my shirt did not rip, but his DNA was there.

ANTONIO TARVER: ONE of my funniest impromptu moments came when I was interviewing Tarver at the post Mosley-De La Hoya II presser. The interview was interrupted when everyone starred at Bob Arum who was at the podium screaming and yelling about the decision being bad and he was out of boxing forever because he felt boxing was corrupt.

When that was over (the video still running) Tarver said "Wow. Can you believe that? Bob Arum out of boxing! Does he always talk like that?" I replied "Only when his fighter loses."

Later in his hotel room celebrating after he beat Jones the first time, I did a tag team interview with Steve Kim and I asked Tarver "were you in there with Roy Jones or RJ?" He laughed and said "Definitely Roy Jones"

BOB ARUM: WHEN I told Bob that Mike Tyson might be making a porno film, he looked disgusted. I asked him if he would see it and he said "No I'm too old for that stuff."

MIKE TYSON: MANY people felt the Lewis-Tyson presser in NYC was shocking and funny but his LA presser to hype his fight with Andrew Golota. His quotes were sensational:

1) When asked what he will bring to the ring, he said "A lot of pain baby!"

2) When asked why he needs to get off his medication before his fight, Tyson said "That's to prevent me from killing you all. You can't believe what you've done to me. It's got my dick all jacked up". People turned around to each other and laughed in shock.

3) When asked what he will do if Golota hits him below, he said "I wish he'd hit me low. I'll hit him back like a motherfucker".

4) When someone asked if he would train at the Kronk Gym in Detroit, Tyson said "Kronk? That's the enemy (meaning E. Steward's camp and his future foe Lennox Lewis and referring to Lewis, 'He thinks he tries to intimidate me, the next time he tries, I'll put a bullet in his motherfucking skull!"

5) MORE TYSON: On my turn, I first asked how he viewed this fight and despite what he has said in the past, I said he wanted to be heavyweight champ again. He said "Really, Listen, I'm a nigger. Listen I don't mean black or white. I mean a street person and I don't particularly like street people. This is who I am but you will never respect me. People will remember me and say 'wasn't that a bizarre individual?'

Later Mike exploded at me. I asked if he was a good friend of Fernando Vargas and if he had visited him before his last fight and if Vargas someone he admired, and what did he say to him before the fight? Tyson replied "I didn't really say anything to him.

I said you have to put him (his opponent) on a stretcher. We don't mean anything malicious about that but fighting is a hurting business and you criticize us for doing our job (getting emotional and yelling) why do you do that? What block have you run? What people have you fought and yet you criticize us? Nigger get of out of boxing if you don't like the game man (I'm white) and he started talking about how attracted he is to boxing and boxers and mentioned he's not gay but he admires fighters.

I asked Mike how he felt about his fight with Golota being called a freak show. I said people feel that here is two fighters with dirty reputations and people may sit back and say who is going to throw the first low blow? Tommy Hearns tried to stop Tyson from answering but Tyson said "That's cool, I'll answer that. How can you judge us? What have you accomplished in your life to judge us and call us freak shows? You're a freak because you are a boxing writer and never fought. You don't even have the nerve to face us? I mean who are you some kind of Italian son ova bitch?"

He asked me to forgive him for his use of cuss words saying he does it all the time. I said "that's ok but I am facing you I'm asking you the questions." Tyson said "No you're not facing me because you're in a boxing field and never fought and never been a champion. Don't you know the sweat and the pain and this is the loneliest fuckin sport in the world? You know what I'm saying? I haven't fucked my wife in a year! You think I give a damn about Andrew Golota? I haven't seen my kids in months!" I asked him why? He said "None of your business white boy but I haven't seen them in months. You think I give a damn about living and dying?

I'm a dysfunctional motherfucker! Come on bring Andrew Golota on! I don't want to beat them I want to strip them of their fucking health. Lennox Lewis? I want him to see pain. I want (my opponents) kids to say when he gets home 'oh daddy are you OK daddy because they don't give a damn about me and my kids". I finally started laughing and said "Yeah what?"

I said "It sounds like you bring a lot of anger in the ring" and Tyson said "Yeah and I like to release it, oh yes I do!"

Tommy Hearns finally broke the exchange saying "That's why it will be a great fight-all that built up anger".

Tyson was asked another question but he still would not let go. You can hear him mutter under his breath "god damn motherfucker asking me a question about boxing and know nothing about it!" after the conference I yelled out to Mike "Hey Mike" and he said "What"? I said "Good luck with the fight I hope you win and he said "Hey Thank you I want to talk more when I get down." He made sure I got to speak with him and let me through the crowd and he shook my hand, apologized to me and said "No hard feeling brother" I said "No hard feelings Mike" I asked "Who would you like to fight next? He said "this is my last fight. I'm tired of this shit. People just want to see me get my butt kicked". I told him "You were a big hit today; if you were a fight commentator you would be great at it". Tyson said "you really think so"? I said "Yes" and he said "Thank you, I wish everyone felt the same way you did".

I asked him about Mike Tyson Records and he responded how happy he felt the way the company was going. Then I said "Mike, do you really deep down like talking to the press?" and he said "Yeah I do. Know why? I'm like a man who likes a woman but she just doesn't like you. You guys will never like me. I'm too much of a nigger for you all".

I asked how confident he was of winning and he said "I'm very confident. I'm right there!" I finally said to him to him "Even though you say you want to retire, it sounds like to me you really don't want to." Tyson replied "I have to retire because they don't want to give me the money and respect so I have to bounce." I asked "Do you think you will ever get that respect?" and he said "Never, I'm a nigger".

That press conference exchange between Tyson and me made the TV and Radio reports-Big Boys, the DJ from Power 106 used the white boy line as part of a promo sound bite. The 'Houseofboxing.com's' Doug Fischer wrote a big story on that. Howard Stern allegedly commented on the conference and aired it on his show. Bob Case, the Vice President of the International Boxing Assn. when he sees me calls me "White boy" in reference of the Tyson exchange. He had said to people on many occasions on how he felt it was the funniest presser he ever saw and marveled at the exchange between Tyson and myself. And actually called Johnny Tapia and told him every line and Tapia thought it was hilarious.

Both Bob Arum and Don King at the time said it was the funniest most bizarre presser they ever saw.

Comedian Chris Rock turned portions of the LA presser into a comedy skit on one of his HBO specials called Tyson for President. One of them involved me.

The announcer says "Vice President Al Gore says he's loyal to his wife and kids. George W Bush tells you the same thing. But isn't that what every presidential candidate will tell you?

Mike Tyson will tell you the truth about his marriage." and they go into the footage of Mike saying "I haven't fucked my wife in a year I haven't seen my kids in months". You hear me ask Why and he said "None of your business white boy but I haven't seen them in months" The announcer comes on again and says "Mike Tyson. He hasn't fucked his wife and it's none of your business white boy. Mike Tyson for President" like a real political commercial!

Later I saw Mike again at the Brewster-Klitschko post fight presser and he remembered me and when I said "May you live to be a thousand years old and the last voice you hear is mine". He said "I'm not ready for that"

Mike's a big fan of a comedian Rudy Ray Moore AKA Dolomite who was a big inspiration to today's rappers and comedians of yesteryear like Richard Pryor, Paul Mooney and others. I asked Mike about Rudy and he said "Oh I love him" he asked me how's Mr. Dolomite doing? I said "He maybe doing a book called Clean Jokes for Church Folks and Tyson said "I don't think that shit will sell".

PUBLICIST JOHN BEYROOTY: Let me say that John is one of the greats in boxing and a legend. He was not too happy with the LA Tyson presser.

A week later, I was at the Ayala-Tapia II post fight presser and after the decision was announced. One of Tapia's people punched Top Rank's Todd Debuef and when I brought that out at the presser which was highly charged. Beyrooty ran from the back of the room to the front and yelled "Don't ever ask another question at a press conference ever again!"

Later Ayala and his wife asked what that was about. People were surprised. He later got back at me at the De LA Hoya-Gatti pre fight presser in LA when I plugged a website I was starting in the middle of asking a question and he pulled the mike on me. Later on, we shared a passion of classic rock music like Leon Russell, the Beatles and others. He was on a tear for a while, even Doug Fischer referred to Beyrooty's treatment of me like a college hazing.

Shortly after the microphone incident, I called John at his office at 6am. Beyrooty gets into work early to deal with the East Coast and overseas foreign press. He answered the phone with a puzzled hello and I said "Hi John, this is Peter Palmiere". John yelled "GOD DAMM IT, IT'S 6 IN THE FUCKIN MORNING. WHAT THE FUCK CAN YOU POSSIBY WANT?" I said "I just wanted to say hello" He replied "GOODBYE" and hung up. We are now on very good terms and he is one of the great publicists in boxing. He should write a book.

HECTOR MACHO CAMACHO: I did a phoner with him and when I mentioned that some people thought Duran beat him in the first fight, Camacho responded that he never heard that. I said Sugar Ray Leonard did. Camacho replied No He didn't and I said Yes he did, I have it on tape and he said it to your face that you got a birthday present that night. He replied "Listen you fuckin asshole; if you think I hate Duran, you must <u>know</u> how much I hate you!"

JAMES TONEY: JAMES and I had many funny encounters. One was in Dan Goosen's office in an interview and he said I should do porno and he could produce and direct it. 'James Lights Out Toney and Dark Gable productions presents Peter Punching Palmiere and the Fat Broads'. I said Yeah? More cushion for Pushin and he said you got that right!

At the Klitschko- Sanders post fight presser, James Toney, egged on by me, got up there and announced it as the James Toney press conference and I asked how he viewed the fight. James said "IT SUCKED. I could have beaten both Klitschko's and Sanders the same night. The German press got mad and heckled him and Toney turned to them and said 'you're all a bunch of Nazis, Sieg Heil Seig Heil' and raised his arm in a Nazi salute!***

WHEN JOSE TORRES original opponent bailed out of a fight at the last minute on 7/14/69 in NYC., Gil Clancy offered to have his fighter Charlie Green fight Torres and Torres agreed. But Green, who was only a fan that evening wasn't aware of the switch.

This was hours before the fight was to happen. Clancy finally found Green eating a hot dog in the stands and said "put down that hot dog, you are fighting tonight" They went into the dressing room and while they were preparing Green for the fight, Green said to Clancy "I'm not fighting till you pay me for my ticket to the fight and my hot dog that you made me throw away". Clancy looked at Green like he was nuts but agreed. The fight lasted two rounds. Green almost put Torres away in the first, but Jose came back to KO Green in the second round. Torres retired after the fight!

Round XI

One Crazy Business

THERE WAS ALWAYS a game that Sue would play, and almost always catch me by surprise. She'd go to the men's cologne department of a major retail outlet to find some samples for her son (and occasionally her car). And at times, without warning she picked up a bottle to test the smell and drenched me with it.

One time I almost got even and grabbed another bottle and took off after her, only to be stopped by a big security guard. Fortunately, although I didn't have an explanation that he believed, I never left the store, so I wasn't charged with shoplifting. Sue also convinced the guard that it was just a game, but I smelled from the stuff she sprayed me with for hours.

WHILE MOST OF the old-timer sports journalists tend to be a bit goofy, I doubt that any could surpass the veteran boxing writer. I have written some pieces on the late Jack Welsh, and recently another old friend, Pat Putnam, climbed the steps into the golden press box in the sky. I couldn't begin to tell you why someone would choose the sport of boxing to write about. In my case it was not only a labor of love but a necessity. It was hard to find a job when I moved to Reno, but it didn't take very long to figure out that while most boxing magazines were located on the East Coast, most fights were based on the West Coast. There was a gap with a clear need to fill, and I jumped in the chasm head first.

Pat Putnam was more than an outstanding writer who certainly belongs in the Hall of Fame, he was my favorite boxing scribe as well. I didn't always agree with him, but he always seemed to make sense in his writings. Pat was the Ring Lardner of his generation, blessed with a great sense of humor and accompanied by an even greater writing talent. Here are a few of the somewhat off the wall things that Pat did/said in his long career in boxing journalism.

- Pat told his wife that he wanted his tombstone to simply read "Keep off the grass". I don't think that happened however.

- There was a time when veteran boxing trainer Rich Giachetti covered scribe Mike Katz with newspapers while Mike was snoozing in a lounge, and Putnam set him on fire. He clearly explained to Mike later that he just wanted to see a Viking funeral. I doubt Katz was amused.

- At a title fight in Las Vegas, popular announcer Mike Buffer was introducing an unending list of celebrity guests, and Pat called out to him "Don't forget Joe DiMaggio," (who wasn't at the fight). Buffer introduced him and the crowd went wild trying in vain, to get a glimpse of the famed 'Yankee Clipper.'

- When his close friend and fellow Marine Bob Waters passed away, Putnam and a few of his writers/drinking buddy friends went to his funeral, and found his coffin completely surrounded by flowers. Never missing a beat, Pat quipped: "Looks like Bob just won the Kentucky Derby."

🏆 In the final pre-fight press conference before his comeback fight with Marvelous Marvin Hagler, promoter Bob Arum requested that there should be 'no more questions about Ray's eyes (he was coming back from a second detached retina). Pat who would always try to comply too any promoters request asked, "Ray, how many fingers am I holding up."

🏆 Pat was in a prisoner of war camp in Manchuria for 17 Months. When asked 'Why he ever surrendered. He coldly answered "I didn't surrender, I was unconscious."

🏆 Putnam lost his nose by driving into a telephone pole, and after he had recovered, he received a bill from the phone company for damaging their property. Pat replied to the phone company that he would gladly pay for it if they would ship him the pole. "That's a pretty expensive souvenir," the guy at the County Clerk's office told him. "I don't want if for a souvenir" Pat replied, "I just want to practice driving around it." He never heard from the phone company again.

🏆 Pat, scribe George Kimball, Angelo Dundee and Mike Katz flew from Baltimore to Miami in 1982, to attend the Pryor/Arguello fight. Between them they managed to finish off the plane's supply of Bloody Marys. Kimball wasn't sure that he would be able to drive. "No problem" Pat said, "I'll drive."

🏆 Kimball recalls that Pat did get them safely to the hotel, but sometime later he realized that he had gone the wrong way out of the Hertz Rental car lot, and drove over a set of steel spikes, puncturing all four of the vehicles tires. They were belted radials and so George drove with the tread-damaged tires for the rest of the weekend.

A FEW TIDBITS ON RELIGION, or simply coincidence, depending on ones belief system, should be included here.

In late August, 1993, after playing a bit of tennis in the hot Northern Nevada sun, I realized that I was quite short of breath after the effort, which I easily attributed to the heat.

The next day my wife Lois had an "executive physical" scheduled for her and me. She was told by a co-worker that I was also eligible for this benefit. The key two letters omitted were that I would be covered only *if* they would find a problem. If not, it would have cost us about $3,000.

Part of the exam was something called a 'heart calcification study', which showed five of my arteries 90% or more blocked. The cardiologist later told me that I wouldn't have made it to year's end, and that was about four months away. A few days later, I had five heart bypasses.

This was clearly something I would not have known about unless I took the physical, which I would not have done, had I known I wasn't covered for it. In short, without some type of miracle or "divine intervention," I would not be writing this book today.

Another interesting aspect of all this was that shortly thereafter they stopped doing the heart calcification study, as they said the test was deemed to be unreliable.

Sue was with me when I went for the results and when I told her I would need the surgery quickly, she went outside the hospital and threw up. She didn't like hospitals and didn't want to lose me (she told me that later) and was afraid of the consequences of the surgery. Her mother Amelia was a former nurse and told her I wouldn't be around very long.

Truth be told, Wuz never visited me in the hospital, although Lois, Eileen, and my oldest son Sean visited often and stayed long. I don't even remember Sue calling, although she may have. Not the kind of memories one prefers to hold on to. But then again, when I returned home, Sue made it a point to pick me up and take me for much needed walks.

Make what you will of this, but to me it was God's way of saying he had other important plans for me. Maybe it was to deal with the problems of others through prayer (Glove2Glove), maybe something else. I don't question the workings of the Lord.

NOT AN ODDITY PER SE, but a great true story about former champ Rudolpho "El Gato/The Cat' Gonzalez. This story, paraphrased here, will be in an upcoming biography.

Rudolfo had been diagnosed with stomach cancer during his pro boxing career and was living in constant agony. He saw three doctors who all gave him less than a year to live. He had a vision of the Lady of Guadalupe, who told him to visit her son. The next day he went into a church and asked Jesus to do with him as he would. When he walked out of the church, the cancer was entirely gone. None of the doctors had any explanation for this miracle. Rudolfo went on to win a world title and is still doing fine today.

MUHAMMAD ALI WAS an introverted 19-year-old Cassius Clay, when he became the first official "trash talker" in boxing and perhaps all professional sports. Where did he get the idea? It was from a guy named George Wagner, whose more common wrestling name was "Gorgeous George."

MY OLD FRIEND THELL TORRENCE, a former top fighter who learned his craft when he worked under the great trainer Eddie Futch has now become an outstanding trainer in his own right, contributes this:

- 🏆 I had a bout scheduled in the Northwest when the promoter switched opponents and chose my stable-mate as my foe.

- 🏆 There are a lot of snakes around the sport of boxing. This brings me to the story of a guy who was walking in the forest and saw an injured snake that was freezing to death. He picked up the snake and put it in a bag. On his way home the snake got his head out of the bag and tried to bite the guy. The guy was disappointed. "Why did you do that? I'm your friend. You were freezing to death and I saved your life." The snake turned and bit him, saying, "Yes, but remember, I'm still a snake".

- 🏆 The moral of the story is choose your friends very carefully. There are many snakes out there, and once a snake, always a snake!

THESE JUICY TIDBITS, COURTESY OF top Midwest promoter Fred Berns, as relayed to me by my friend David Ruff, who also adds a few.

- 🏆 Walter Cowans was a junior middleweight from Milwaukee. He was a well-known professional opponent. Fred Berns was supposed to have him on his show in Gary, Indiana. Walter was late to the fight in Gary and Fred tried to call him, to no avail.

- 🏆 It seemed that while driving on the way to Gary, after a couple of hours, Walter gets to the toll booth. The toll taker notices Cowans is smoking a joint and notifies Indiana state police. They notify Fred, and there was no fight for Walter Cowans that night. Fred was also unable to find an opponent to replace Cowans.

🏆 In Minneapolis, Fred was waiting in his hotel room at the Majestic Star one night. He hears a bunch of racket outside around 2:30 a.m., hollering, screaming, cursing, etc. Fred ignores this and remains in bed for a couple of hours before he finally gets up. He's thinking the racket was from the guests or fighters he's promoting on the card. He looks down the balcony and at poolside; there are some lounge chairs and a table. Here was Walter Cowans arguing with himself! Fred was a bit shocked; but Cowans did end up fighting that night in Minneapolis.

HEAVYWEIGHT DICKIE "RAGING BULL" RYAN was a highly sought after athlete in his high-school days. He was recruited by University of Nebraska's football head coach. The coach himself went to recruit Ryan. One week, Ryan runs into Bruce "The Mouse" Strauss. Strauss than relates to Ryan about all his boxing endeavors, and also tells Ryan how he could make a lot of money in boxing. He puts Ryan in the Nebraska Golden Gloves a week later. Ryan wins the tournament and becomes the Golden Gloves heavyweight champ. A week after that, Strauss puts Ryan in his first pro fight. Ryan wins the pro debut. Berns now believes that Strauss must really be able to communicate to people, to convince them to fight one week in the Golden Gloves, and to turn pro the following week. Strauss must really have the gift of gab.

Ron Branch was fighting early in his pro career, in 1974, at the Steelworkers Hall in Baltimore. The crowd was big for such a small venue. A boxer was shadow boxing in the hall with his gloves and robe on, getting ready to make his entrance into the arena. He was still shadow boxing going down the hallway to the ring. The fighter climbs up into the ring and goes through the ropes, still shadow boxing. The handlers take his robe off, to find out that he has no clothes on at all--no cup, no underwear, no trunks, just shoes. The crowd goes crazy, and the guy is still shadow boxing in the ring. All of a sudden a group of Baltimore police storm the ring and come up with a robe

One Crazy Business

and escort him out of the ring, to the hallway and then to the dressing room. His nights action ended very quickly, without him even fighting.

THIS STORY INVOLVES fight announcer/writer Larry Tornambe. Larry had one pro fight for David Ruff, his promoter, and it was by accident.

"I had a middleweight named Herbie Chapman, who was supposed to fight David Moyer in Reading, Pennsylvania, at the Rivers Edge Hotel. I couldn't find Herbie all day. I was frantic, calling his friends, his father. Everyone was mad at the promoter (myself), matchmaker, and his father. Herbie's father had sold $500 worth of tickets. He was so mad because he couldn't find his son. So he said, "To hell with the fight and the $500."

I was calling fighters left and right trying to find a replacement. Then I thought of Larry. Larry was out of work at the time. He said, "Give me an hour." He had to go to the store. I called him back in an hour, and he decided to take the fight. We go to Reading, Larry makes weight, starts out good in the fight, and gets stopped in round three. Larry ended his boxing career that quickly--his one and only pro fight.

DAVID RUFF ADDS THIS: Veteran New England boxing maven Dick Kelly took a job at a racetrack in Brockton, Mass. He asks for two security guards, and without him knowing, they give him Tom McNeely, former heavyweight contender, and Paul Pender, former middleweight champion. Dick got the shock of his life after finding out who they were.

They're making their rounds, and they run into three young drunks. Dick gives a bag of money to the bartender and tells him to hold it. Tom McNeely and Paul Pender try to get the guys out of the bar in the racetrack. The young guys didn't know who they were dealing with. So they told McNeely and

Pender they were going to "get their asses kicked." The young guys bravely laughed when making the threats.

Dick Kelly tells them that they don't know who they're dealing with; they say yes we do, just two dumb security guards. Pender hits one guy; down he goes. The other two guys go after McNeely. They tell Tom that he's in for the beating of his life.

McNeely throws a one-two, and down goes the first guy. Then he throws another one-two, and down goes the second guy.

Dick Kelly remembers about the money, so he asks McNeely, "Do you have the bag of money?" McNeely says no. He asks Pender, who also says no. Finally he remembers he gave it to the bartender, and he runs up to him. He says, "Do you still have that bag I gave you?" The bartender says yes. The bartender asks, "What's in the bag, Dick?" He says, "About $100,000."

All in all, the track still had their $100,000, and three drunks go out on their butts, never knowing who they were dealing with.

ANOTHER RUFF STORY: In 1986, in York, Pennsylvania, I had taken a group of fighters to the Sheraton Hotel in York. Not knowing that the group "Live" was going to be performing onstage before the fight, I told my fighters that I didn't know who these people were, who were singing in a little side bar in the Hotel. Even the famous fighters didn't know who they were either. But three years later the group was to become famous.

That same year (1986), I took a group of fighters to West Chester High School in Pennsylvania, and the rock group "Hooters" was playing before the fights. Nobody knew who Hooters was either. About three years later they also would become famous. Rock groups and boxing do seem to mix!

RUFF CONTINUES: IN 1995, while in rehab at Bisell Hospital in Hockessin, Delaware, most of the staff there were excited to find out that I was a boxing manager.

My fighter Greg Hackett, 39, from Chester, Pennsylvania, was making a comeback. So being housed at a state rehab center for my neck problems, the staff would always keep the payphone open for me, so that I would be able to make matches for Greg.

I set up a fight for Greg to fight Larry Graham in Harrisburg, Pennsylvania, at the Holiday Inn. The state rehab decided to release me for the bout. So, I drove there with a friend, John Thomas, and Greg Hackett and some other fighters, in John's truck.

The State had to ask my fighters whether I was coming back before morning, since I was going to Harrisburg that evening. Yeah, I came back quickly that night, because the fight card started at 9. Greg went on at about 9:30, scored a second-round knockout of Larry Graham, and I was back at Bissell by 12:30 a.m.

CONCERNING MILLS LANE, Reno's great referee and famous Judge with a television show, the City itself now has a Street called "Mills Lane," and I'm not sure just when that occurred.

A number of years back I was asked to participate in a roast for Mills, to raise money for multiple sclerosis. I gave him a gift, a black bra, and told him it was to cover the glare coming off his shaved head, which everyone who watched boxing had to deal with. He accepted in good naturedly.

DAVE NEWHOUSE, OUTSTANDING California Bay Area boxing writer adds this gem: "In the mid 60's at the Oakland Auditorium, Roger Rischer was schedule to fight Willie Richardson for the California State Heavyweight championship. As the referee was giving instructions, Rischer said something to Richardson, which angered Willie and he responded by kicking Rischer. Rischer took off after Richardson who ran through the ropes around the ring and into the street, with Rischer close behind.

The California State title had to be put on hold for another time.

LOU DUVA PROVIDES another quote on his heavyweight, big punching contender Samuel Peter: "If fists could talk, then Sam would win spelling bees."

FROM ERIC ARMIT, UK Historian and Scribe: British boxing journalist and broadcaster Reg Gutteridge was sharing a dinner table with Sonny Liston back in the days when Liston was world champion and the most feared man in boxing. Liston was boasting to Reggie about how tough he was and Reg became a little tired of hearing this. Finally he interrupted Liston, picked up a fork from the table and said to Liston, "If you are so tough then let me see you do this." Reg then raised the fork and with all of his might stabbed it into his leg. Liston, as well as all those present was shocked and if it had been possible he would have blanched at this, but what Sonny did not know was that Reg lost his leg at the Normandy landings and the leg he 'stabbed' was an artificial limb.

"IRISH" PAT LAWLOR, Popular Bay Area fighter, has one ambition right now, to fight a world champion in every weight division from featherweight up.

As of this writing, all he needs is a bout with a former heavyweight champ to meet this unusual goal. That would be a record worthy of any Trivial Pursuit question.

Pat was with his girlfriend Tiana and was set to fight Roberto Duran, who was a bit past his prime, in Panama. Pat met and married a young lady who was interested in becoming an American citizen. After finding out that this lass was using him, he divorced her and is now back with Tiana, who understood and generously forgave his transgression.

FROM JACKIE KALLEN one of boxings great ladies, this gem:

One of my favorite boxing stories is about a conversation that took place in my office at the gym. Several of the fighters were sitting around discussing whether or not sex before a fight is harmful. One guy said, "I give up all sex for at least a week before a fight. I don't even touch a woman. It drains your testosterone."

A second guy pipes up, "I give it up at least a month before a fight. I don't even touch a woman. It drains your testosterone."

The third guy said, "I give it up for six weeks before a fight. I don't even touch a woman. I just masturbate every night."

GEORGE FOREMAN MADE this great quote on HBO TV.

"Today's champions are tomorrow's contenders". Big George got that one 100 percent correct.

JULIAN EGET, PRESIDENT of the Golden State Boxers Association chimes in with this one.

I remember seeing a heavyweight fighter who was a big puncher, but I didn't know if he could take a punch or not. He had a fight one night and his manager told him that, if he had any kind of a problem, to look in the corner and he'd tell him what to do.

He looked pretty good in the first round, then in round two, from out of nowhere comes a right hand and my fighter goes down. He's dazed and looking in the corner. His manager keeps screaming "Get up at eight, get up at eight." My fighter looks at his manager and asks "What time is it now?"

And Julian will never forget the last words Art Aragon heard when fighting Carmen Basilio. It was the referee counting: 101, 102, 103.

ICE JOHN SCULLY from his upcoming book "The Iceman Diaries":

My professional boxing debut was slated for September 16, 1988 at the Hartford Civic Center and I was very excited about it as you can imagine. It was like a whole new world I was entering, joining the ranks of all the guys I watched on TV for so many years.

Now I had something in common with the guys I looked up to: I was a professional boxer just like they were. If I had any apprehension at all it was about the fact that the game I was entering into was much different from the amateur boxing that I was now so accustomed to. You see, amateur boxing is also a very dangerous sport and people can get knocked out and cut and punch drunk just like they can in the pros. The major difference between the two levels, though, was made crystal clear to me many times by Hartford's legendary old trainer, Johnny Duke.

Duke is the type of guy that is, let's say a no-nonsense individual—always very direct and to the point. Duke makes Mickey from the "ROCKY" movies look like Mister Rogers by comparison. He is a member of the National Golden Gloves Hall of Fame, Duke ran the Bellevue Square Boys Club in the Bellevue Square housing projects in Hartford, CT. for something like forty years. He has always been a real straight shooting type of old school Italian guy, the kind of guy that could use the "N" word in the cities toughest project without anyone even batting an eye. The type of guy that could swear more in one hour than most sailors could in a month. The type of guy who could have walked through the city during the race riots of the late 1960's and get from one end to the other without anyone even so much as raising their voice to him. The type of guy that would pull his truck over on a busy street and stop traffic so he could get out and pick up a discarded winter coat off the street and bring it back to "the square" and give it to someone that didn't have one.

So if there was anyone that would tell it to me straight (not that I even wanted to know) in regard to the reality of professional boxing it was Johnny Duke. When I was an amateur he used to tell me, *"You know what's going to happen when you turn pro? Now, as an amateur, when you get a little nick under your eye, the referee and your Mommy and your F****** coach come running and want to know if your OK. They say 'Is he OK? We better stop it so he doesn't get hurt. Let's get him a F*****' bandage. But when your a pro and you get a big F****** gash under your eye you know what your opponents trainer tells him to do? He tells him to go out and bust your other F***** eye open for you, that's what!"*

BENNIE GEORGINO, HALL of Fame promoter and boxing good guy, tells this true story of a title fight he promoted in Miami Beach in the early 1980's.

My fighter, Alberto Davila was fighting for the bantamweight title during hurricane season. Davila was losing badly after five rounds and I told him if he didn't knock his opponent out in the next round, I was stopping the fight.

That motivated Davila and as the rain began to fall and the bell rang to start round six, Davila came out, and like a tiger, knocked his opponent out.

After the bout, a reporter asked me how I motivated Davila, and I told him, "It wasn't me that motivated him, it was the holy water falling from the sky.

At that point the hurricane hit full blast and took with it the ring, and everything surrounding it.

Round XII
The Final Bell

MY TIMESHARE IN Las Vegas provided Sue and I with many weird and yet wonderful, never to be forgotten moments, but in fairness it wasn't always just her goofiness that was the issue.

Both Wuz and I had/have bad eyesight, and are almost blind without our glasses. One night, at the timeshare, I got up early to take some meds while she was still in bed fast asleep. I sat down by the table (it was still dark), and crunch, there went her glasses, which she had stupidly put on a chair.

The frames were crushed and both of the lenses had come out. I knew that there was going to be a major problem, so I waited until sunrise and woke her up to tell her what happened and be prepared for the insults that I knew would be coming.. "You fucking asshole," she shouted (it was always her favorite term of endearment towards me), "These are your glasses." Whoops! I looked at them in the daylight now, and she was correct. Why would have I put the glasses in such a stupid place? That would have been a Woozel thing.

I asked Sue to go with me to the nearby mall because I didn't have a back-up pair of glasses on hand but Sue, still a bit upset with me for waking her up for nothing, refused to go. So when the mall opened a few hours later, I slowly squinted and walked the ½ mile or so to the mall, made my way up the escalator and with the help of Lenscrafters, had my glasses repaired.

Now, with my glasses sitting securely on my nose, I knew getting back to the timeshare would be very easy. It was, until I reached the final step of the mall escalator, stepped off a bit early, and fell over a large cactus plant. Fortunately, there was no damage to myself or the plant. Although the security guard standing there was more than a little shocked.

SUE WAS ALWAYS tasting food in the supermarkets. She had a particular interest in gingerroot, and she would always break off a piece of the bitter plant and eat it, saying it was good for her digestion and breath. Maybe it was, but it certainly didn't do much help prevent her colon cancer.

I recall the time when Sue's girlfriend, Tracey sent her a birthday card, and she wrote on it, "to my best *fiend*." We had plenty of laughs over that one.

While the final years of Sue's life, after she was diagnosed with the cancer, were still mostly fun and we both truly believed that with a lot of prayers, treatment (alternative medicine) along with the radiation and standard chemotherapy, we could beat this ugly disease! God has his agenda and his own reasons for doing things, and it just didn't work out that way for us. The miracle we prayed for never happened. It was at this stage that Sue said her infamous words: "I can't die now. I haven't spent all my money yet." Sadly she never did get to spend it.

A classic example of "Woozel logic" was shown before the 2004 Presidential election. She asked me who I favored and why, and I told her John Kerry for a variety of reasons, most of all, that he was a true military hero, which I felt we needed to make America safe.

Wuz agreed with my views or said that he did, but shortly afterwards she told her husband Jack to vote on Election Day for George Bush. Why? Because his tax break enabled them to get back more money then they would have otherwise. Never mind that the President was making his rich friends richer and taking from the poor to do so. Sue didn't she didn't like Bush's policies in Iraq. Still, the right thing for her to do was tell Jack to vote for the incumbent. Sadly that type of logic is pretty much the same for most American voters. Like Sue, don't bother to check out or pay attention to the big picture, vote for the man who gives you the most money back.

ABOUT FIVE YEARS before she passed away she bravely faced the few options she was given; Sue didn't want to go the surgery route. She was much too vain to wear a colostomy bag although she had to know it would have made no difference to those of us who loved her and needed her around, and only God knows if that would have really made any difference in prolonging her life. So together we looked for some other viable answers, but obviously no workable ones were ever found.

The doctors never seemed to bother to suggest trying experimental drugs which may or may not have prolonged her life. Looking back, I think this was because an oncologist's office is now little more than a revolving door and there are just too many patients for the cancer doctors to handle and keep track of. That's a sad commentary on our times.

First Sue tried the radiation route and did take the maximum amount her body was able to handle. I met her at the radiologist almost every time she went, and believe me that event wasn't easy for either one of us. While the radiologist's office wasn't very far from my house, I always felt tired (I was later diagnosed with anemia) and had no idea why. I accompanied Wuz on almost all of her medical visits, except the mandatory evaluation x-rays, which she didn't need me there for, unless we were going out to eat and/or gamble afterwards. Sue wasn't very well versed in medical terminology and in my youth I, at one time worked in a pharmacy and was fairly familiar with most of the terms, certainly the older ones, although I can't say I was familiar with most of the newer medications. She did want me to explain what all the things the doctor had written on the x-ray report said. Besides, knowing and without acknowledging to her that she may have been nearing the end, I wanted to be at her side as much as possible. Anyone who has gone through this experience knows that there can never be enough time left to be together. I didn't want to lose her, she meant so much to me. But I didn't want to see her in constant pain either, knowing that there was no hope.

The final two years of Sue's life were very hard, not only on her, but on those of us who loved her deeply. She rarely complained, even till the end, and most of the memories I have of those days were not fun, but very painful. Those are the memories that as much as I don't want to remember, I still do. But Wuz was hanging tough and only complained to me the last few weeks of her life, and even then she was able to teach everyone around her how to die with dignity.

In fact, during the final year her health became so bad that she would rarely make it to thrift stores, something she had always loved to do, and now these visits there had become very few and far between. Wuz didn't have enough energy to bake Christmas cookies or the Kailua cake to take to our many friends as gifts, with cards signed "Merry Christmas," Love, Rusty & Susiey. The baking of the cookies and the signing and delivery of the cards had been a long standing tradition with us.

For her final birthday present, I reserved a small cottage for two days and a condo for one, up at Lake Tahoe. Lois accompanied me on the first day and Sue stayed with me for the last two. We went to the Tahoe Biltmore for breakfast, and the restaurant was located downstairs in the hotel/casino. Wuz got down okay, but found that going back up was almost impossible. She was coughing constantly and out of breath. It didn't take a rocket scientist to know that she didn't have a lot of time left on this Earth.

But one important thing Wuz did do was to make damn sure that Joe, the scumbag who beat her up and almost killed her, and was now going on trial for beating up another woman, was not going to walk away free. He had hurt enough innocent people. For some unexplainable reason, Joe decided to use Sue as a character witness in that trial. How stupid could he be? Using a woman he beat up and had left for dead, as a character witness was dumb,

Instead of lying for him, particularly when there were police photos of the way he had left her. Him, and giving positive testimony about this cold-blooded thug, to the judge, Sue allowed the pictures of what he had done to her to be brought before the court, and Joe was put away for the maximum sentence, which, although not as long as I feel it should have been, should have made some women breathe easier for a short time. She also found out that Joe now had Crones Disease, so what goes around does indeed come around.

It was during that time, and knowing full well that her own time on this earth was growing short, Sue came out with another of her right on expression "Life sucks, death sucks, nothing's right!" For her, at that moment in time, nothing could have been more truthful.

IN LATE 2001, a little more then two years before she was to pass away, Sue called me from home and told me that her mother, Amelia, whose home Sue was living in at the time, was in a lot of pain and asked that I arrived at her house and help get her to the hospital. I drove to her mom's house in Northwest Reno, quickly evaluated the situation, and called 911. An ambulance was dispatched and they took Amelia to the hospital, where, after waiting a few hours with her and Sue in the emergency room at Washoe Medical Center, the doctor on call at the time, badly misdiagnosed her with a bad shoulder sprain, put her arm in a sling, and had me take her home.

It was remarkable that a shoulder sprain was diagnosed for an elderly lady who wasn't able to get off the gurney to get to the bathroom? That was a totally incompetent doctor. This guy must have gotten his degree from NYU (New York Unemployment). In fairness to the doc, the emergency room was packed, but that's still no excuse.

Once we returned to her mom's house, it was impossible, even for me, to lift her up the small step to her front door, as my bad back couldn't handle her weight. Then I told Sue to get on the phone and have her mom's orthopedic doctor call 911 and have her admitted to the hospital where she would be diagnosed by a 'real doctor' The ambulance returned and took Amelia to the hospital, where they took x-rays and found that she had a fractured hip. Talk about your chance for a classic malpractice suit, but one was never filed. No wonder Amelia was screaming for help and wouldn't let anyone touch her. Sadly, except for a brief visit, Amelia was never to return to her home.

I vividly recall the anger I felt when the gal who answered the phone at the ambulance company asked Wuz why Amelia was screaming. Sue handed me the phone and taking it I said, "Because she's having a fucking wonderful time dealing with the morons in the emergency room, and can't wait to see them again. She's enjoying the great weather today, waiting for your guys to get their lazy asses up here." Talk about your stupid ass questions. The ambulance crew arrived and did their usual fine job, but the office help left a lot to be desired.

Amelia was then in her late 80's and quickly went downhill from there, putting more stress and aggravation on Wuz than she needed. Amelia went from the local hospital to a Reno nursing home. Then Sue's brother Jinx took their mom to a nursing home near his home in St. George, Utah, where she suffered a stroke and was taken off life support by her brother, with the consent of the entire family and in accordance with her mother's wishes.

Sue was at the nursing home when Jinx picked Amelia up, and told me after he left Reno that she knew that she would never see her mom alive again. She was right, except for the ashes she always carried around.

And quickly, with the loss of her beloved mother, it became Sue's turn to start going downhill. Wuzzel loved her mother very much and was constantly crying out for her after her passing, missing her greatly.

That stress, plus her somewhat misguided belief that her brother had sold her home (her mom's actually) out from under her, caused her stress, and that probably helped bring on the cancer again, big time. Amelia left no will, and that may also have been part of Sue's downhill health problems as it resulted stress caused by the contested ownership of the house. Of course, there were also a number of other contributing factors to Wuz's rapid decline in health.

SUE HAD ALWAYS looked up to her older brother Jinx, and the two of them really went at it when she found out that he was going to be selling their mothers house. In truth, the house was much too large for Sue and Jack, who didn't need three bedroom and, high utility bills, but that logic didn't seem to matter much to her at the time. That house and the memories it held within, was one of the few things that she felt kept her close to her mother. Truth be told, if Sue would have lived there a few more months, it would have saved her the extra stress and trouble of having to buy a mobile home in a less desirable area. She said often that she didn't want to become "trailer trash."

Again, in truth, Sue could and should have taken better care of herself--much better. It's not a good idea to stay out or up all night when you have an extremely compromised immune system. But Wuz had always lived life on her own terms, usually on the edge, and that wasn't going to change until she became too weak, and with no other choice, she have to slow down.

The fact that she also had a Grand Mal seizure and had to take even more meds (they put her on a blood thinner) didn't help either. It meant adding another pill to her regimen, which in the last two or three months she couldn't get straight anyhow (she had to take morphine for the pain) causing memory loss, and soon thereafter she began to lose a lot of weight and energy. On a few occasions she took too much of a blood thinner and I had to get her a transfusion of vitamin K, in the emergency room. She simply could no longer keep track of what pills to take and when to take them. It was indeed a tough time for her and those of us who loved her. Needless to say, the worst feeling of all was the helplessness. Watching a loved one day is never easy, but not being able to say or do anything to make her smile or a bit more comfortable was very frustrating to this old guy.

I helped in finding Sue and Jack a mobile home in Sun Valley, north of town, but Sue kept saying how much she hated the place and that there was no grass there for her pit bull Jinx to play in. She also continued to cry for her mother a lot. I do believe that they are now together forever, in a far better place.

THE LAST FUN TRIP (he showed her goofiness on was when we took was to the World Boxing Hall of Fame in Los Angeles, in October of 2002. Sue had lost some weight and didn't have very much energy, but she still wanted to go, and as I had always enjoyed her company, I figured it would do us both some good to get away and take her mind off her pain as well as her mom's passing.

We arrived at the Reno Airport, where I passed through security with no problem at all. Sue was right behind me and when she went through the metal detector every alarm in the place went off, or so it seemed. We were quickly surrounded by armed security guards, with their weapons pointed directly at us. They asked me if I was with her, I said yes and they told me to sit down and wait, as I had passed the screener with no problem.

"What did Wuz do now?" I wondered to myself. Security guards were walking past, looking at me strangely, and shaking their heads in utter disbelief as if to say, "He's with her? What's wrong with him?" type of expressions on their face.

Airport security, when they found out I was with Sue, asked (ordered) me to not move from my designated seat, so I couldn't really see what was going on. Suddenly I heard some very loud laughing, and not just from Wuz. What she had in her carry-on bag was (1) a very long, sharp kitchen knife that she brought with her to do her toenails as she explained, (2) a silver metal flask of brown liquid (Jack Daniels), and (3) a lab test tube full of grey matter (her mother's ashes). When security asked what was in the vial, Sue shook it (probably scaring everyone watching) responded. "Oh, that's my mother," and then shaking the test tube again in their direction said, "Say hello to mom."

Security knew no one could intentionally be that goofy and after confiscating the knife, they let her pass with the rest of her oddball goodies, including me.

BUT SADLY IT WAS all downhill for her from then on. Wuz began losing weight and energy. The last two months she was actually telling me and others, on occasion, that she wanted to die.

The last movie that we saw together, strangely enough, was a remake of the first movie that we saw together, "The Texas Chainsaw Massacre." I don't care for those kinds of macabre pictures, although Sue always liked them. I didn't want to go to that movie and Sue said she'd meet me at the movie complex earlier to see a different picture. But by the time she arrived there (she later acknowledged my allegation that it was intentional), the only movie to see at that time was the remake. So we saw it, and she loved it. At least I was glad to be able to make her happy, although this time it really wasn't intentional.

She was in and out of the hospital on a regular basis after that, having some hallucinations, probably at times from improper use of the oxygen and morphine she now had to use all of the time, and also from the other medications, but Wuz still kept her sense of humor almost until the very end.

I remember a day when she was in her bed at Washoe Medical Center, and I went to visit her. I brought along a boxing friend, a gal who often worked the corners at fights, Brandie Lee, who Sue said that she had never met before, to the hospital to wish her well, and we went up first, while my wife Lois parked the car.

I walked into her room first, and there was a nurse in there talking with her. Wuz was sitting up, saw me and said, "I want you to meet my best friend Rusty and this is his wife Lois." Then she looked at Brandie a second time and said, "You're not Lois, who the hell are you?" We all cracked up laughing.

About a month before she passed away I took Wuz to her insurance company and the DMV to get her drivers license renewed, since she had made up her mind to drive no matter what the doctor said. Being on morphine she was not supposed to do that, and probably rarely if ever, used her renewed license much, if at all.

I picked Sue up from the hospital a few weeks before her passing and took her to her sister's house. Marion was going to take care of her, or try to. On the way there Sue was experiencing a few hallucinations. But I got her to her sister's okay, and then went with Marion to Sue's trailer to pick up her oxygen tank and have her son carted off to jail (Dorian would never show up at his Parole Officer) for doing drugs and other things at the house, which he had turned into a hotel and laundry mat for what seemed to be all the losers who lived in the area.

By the time Marion returned to her home with the oxygen, which we should have taken, but forgot to pick up on our first trip up there, Sue may have lost too much oxygen to the brain because all that evening she was talking to herself and wandering around her sister's house, and Marion had to go to work the next day. So, we were left with little choice but to take Sue back to the hospital the next day, for the last time.

A DAY OETWO BEFORE THAT, I met with Wuz at a local casino, the Gold Dust West to be exact, expecting to discuss another problem that she was having with her son, Dorian, who was out of jail and living with her. It was a problem which really never got discussed since she was then taking heavy doses of morphine, which I didn't know about at the time. And she wouldn't have even been driving, if I would have known. She wanted to take a final ride to Boomtown, another casino about seven miles further out, and a place where we spent many a fun night.

Sue got into my car and we drove the seven miles to the casino. But when we got there she barely had the energy to make the short walk inside, and when she did, she just plopped down on a stool at the nearest slot machine we could find. This once gorgeous, very healthy specimen of femininity had grown very frail.

After resting for about five minutes Wuz told me she felt like she was going to throw up and she wanted to go home. I left her in the casino, got the car and picked her up at the nearest exit, and on the way back to the hospital, she was bending over in my car's passenger's seat, in pain, yelling that she wanted to die. Needless to say, seeing her like this tore me to pieces, although I wasn't about to show it to her. But she knew, that after 25 years, how could she not?

I got her to the hospital and did my best O J Simpson running through the airport routine, with her sitting in the wheelchair I was pushing to the third floor oncology ward. When we got there, they gave her some meds, took out an infected port in her chest, and asked me to take her home, which I did. She wasn't going to be able to drive anymore in this lifetime.

The next day I took Wuz to the oncologist's office, where she was in great pain and said again that she wanted to die. The nurse from the office called me at home the next morning and told me she had seen a lot of these type of cancer cases and that I should prepare myself, the end was growing near for my Wuzzel. I spent about two weeks of almost non-stop crying. I was on one hand glad that she would finally be out of her pain, but sad because I knew that my days of serious joy and laughter were about to end. I knew that I'd be very lonely and that Sue was very special, a one-of-a-kind human being who gave me the greatest times in my life.

A few days later Sue was admitted into Washoe Med for the final time. She knew it was over, and with the strong medication she was on, was pretty much out of it to the end. But when she first checked in, she wrote on the bulletin board in her hospital room. "Please come in to let me thank you for your kindness." It was for the nurses, and sadly it was all too obvious that Sue knew it would be over very soon.

FOUR DAYS BEFORE she passed away, on a Sunday, Sue had her husband Jack call me in the morning and she got on the phone and said to me in a voice as strong as I heard in a long time, "What the hell are you doing at home, asshole? Get your fat, lazy ass down here now, and bring me some food."

I hoped that maybe the miracle I was constantly praying for had indeed happened. I brought the food and got there quickly. And Wuz was sitting up in bed reading the newspaper, and she remained very strong for four hours before the pain reached her again. She no longer could eat after that day, but I knew full well that those four hours were her way of saying goodbye to me. However, she had to know that I would be there, by her side with her every day until the end.

Sue passed away at age 54, at about five a.m., on Feb. 19, 2004, and something very special went out of my life, perhaps forever, laughter. I know her passing was for the best, as she was in an enormous amount of pain, constantly, and had no chance to recover, but I'd be lying if I wrote that I didn't want "the old Woozel" back with me. Even now, more than two years after her passing, I have days when I can't stop the tears from flowing.

God willing, maybe in the next life, and in future lifetimes we will be together again. What a blessing that would be. In fact I look forward to it. I have to. If ever two people were meant to be together through eternity, it was Sue and I. In my belief system, I feel that all the special people in your life who were with you before will join you in a future life, although we obviously have no memory of the past lives. I was with Wuz as often as possible (although it was very hard emotionally on me) in her final days, and I don't know how much I cried over losing her. Her oncologist's nurse had called me again and told me that she could no longer eat and didn't have much time left. Time became little more then a blur after that, and I was just going through the motions. I never realized just how much I loved that woman.

AS MUCH AS WE had bugged her about doing it, Sue left no will. After her passing, it was left to her older sister Marion, Marion's fiancée Paul, and me pretty much, to take care of Sue's last wishes, which gratefully, Marion assumed most of the responsibility for. I was/am limited by two torn rotator cuffs and arthritis in my neck, back and knees, the last two old football injuries that have caught up to me in recent years. In fact, I no longer drive.

Perhaps the hardest thing that Marion had to do was put Sue's pit bull down. Jinx was nine years old, with ongoing health problems, and simply wouldn't get along with one of her dogs, as Marion tried her best to keep Jinx (the dog, not the brother) as she believed it was what Sue would have wanted. I', not sure about that, as Sue wanted Jinx with her in Heaven.

I would have taken Jinx (Sue's dog) if she got along with our dog, Muey, but they hated each other, so it was a moot point. Personally, I liked Jinx, but she would have been hard to take care of, and now I know she's with Sue again in Heaven, with Sue where she truly belongs, and where we will all be together again very soon.

We did adopt a young (about a year old) rotweiller cross, female, who had given birth to a litter of six pups in the shed in Sue's backyard. When Marion had found the dogs they were starving and near death. Marion was able to get rid of the pups,

The Final Bell

(adopted) and we took the dog that turned out to be a very smart, loving animal, and gave new energy to Muey, our old Chesapeake/Labrador cross, not to mention to our household. We named the dog "Ting," because it looked like "some *ting*" other then her real name, which was Ashley. Her name is now "Binky" because that's the noise her tail makes constantly.

I BELIEVE THAT SUE has visited me twice thus far since her passing. About a week after she passed away I heard a sharp buzzing in my ear, which didn't last long. I looked at the clock and it was 3 a.m., the same time she used to wake me up in the hotels, saying, "Turn over asshole, you're snoring." And she'd toss an ashtray my way, or put pretzels or peanut shells in my bed when I went to the bathroom. At times she'd get out of bed, hide by the side of the bathroom door, and when I came out of the bathroom, almost scare the life out of me. That was Sue. It was always playtime, well, almost always.

Wuz loved late night snacks. In fact, I can't begin to count how many times she woke me and asked if there was a candy machine on the hotel floor, and eventually one of us had to get up and look for it, usually me, because she never wore anything under her thin nightgown, and would have been a very inviting target for some would-be rapist.

The second visit was in a dream, and although I can't remember exactly what she said, I remember us talking together. Was it real? I believe it was. Sue told me she was doing okay and not to worry. I wish she said she'd be waiting for me. Then again, maybe she did. I certainly am going to believe that until the day I die, and hopefully much longer.

I've dreamed about Wuz a lot since then, but I dreamed about her a lot before she passed away also, so I can't honestly count that as visitations.

I don't worry, it's not my style. But I do miss her and love her very much and I know I always will. Lois understands my feelings and knows that no one can ever make me relax and laugh the way Sue did.

Even as I now write this, almost two years after her passing, I still get emotional when I talk about or think of her at times. Sue is/was, and always will be, a huge part of my life. I'm crying now as I finish this final editing.

Her husband Jack got a visit from Susiey as well, in a dream. And, strangely enough, a separate visit from Jinx, her pit bull.

Sue also visited her sister. Marion was lying in her backyard one evening and asked Sue for a sign that she was okay. Suddenly, across the heavens, came a shooting star. Sue was going to tell all of us, in her own way, like she always did, that she was doing just fine.

Dorian, with his girlfriend at that time, along with Marion and her daughter Adrian, and Lois and I went to scatter her and her dog Jinx's ashes, in the same cemetery where her mom's and dad's cremated remains are interred. It was about five months after Sue had passed away and we were all very teary eyed. All I could say was "we're only on this Earth for a short time, but love is eternal. Sue will always be here with us." And I have no doubt that she will be.

Rest in peace, Sue, as you're in Heaven now, where you rightfully belong. God willing all your loved ones, myself included, will be joining you again for many more lifetimes of fun and adventure. For this lifetime your ship has sailed off, leaving me and others having to learn how to laugh and enjoy life all over again. My ship is still anchored, but I know that soon I'll be off to join you in a better place. You alone now how much that means to me.

As of now, the sun still rises in the Eastern sky, but it's just not as bright as it was when you were here. The stars still twinkle in the sky, but there seem to be far fewer than before. I really miss you Sue, and I will always!

Forever!

Printed in the United States
72922LV00003B/109-114